Cool Tricks & Hot Tips for
Adobe Premiere Elements 2018
A Muvipix.com Guide
by Steve Grisetti

A step-by-step guide to creating 50 cool special
effects with – and dozens of hot tips for mastering –
Adobe's best-selling video editing program.

Want to see our tricks in action?

Check out our Cool Tricks & Hot Tips page at Muvipix.com. We'll show you examples of some of the effects we create in this book as well as walk you through the process of creating a few more, step-by-step.

http://Muvipix.com/CoolTricks2018.php

About Muvipix.com

Muvipix.com was created to offer support and community to amateur and semi-professional videomakers. Registration is free, and that gets you access to the world's friendliest, most helpful forum and lots of ad-free space for displaying your work. On the products page, you'll find dozens of free tips, tutorials, motion backgrounds, DVD templates, sound effects, royalty-free music and stock video clips. For a small annual subscription fee that we use to keep the site running, you'll have unlimited downloads from the ever-growing library of support materials and media.

We invite you to drop by and visit our thriving community. It costs absolutely nothing – and we'd love to have you join the neighborhood!

http://Muvipix.com

About the author

Steve Grisetti holds a master's degree in Telecommunications from Ohio University and spent several years working in the motion picture and television industry in Los Angeles. A veteran user of several video editing programs and systems, Steve is the co-founder of Muvipix.com, a help and support site for amateur and semi-professional videomakers. A professional graphic designer and video freelancer, he has taught classes in Photoshop, lectured on design and even created classes for lynda.com. He lives in suburban Milwaukee.

Other books by Steve Grisetti

Adobe Premiere Elements 2.0 In a Snap (with Chuck Engels)
Cool Tricks & Hot Tips for Adobe Premiere Elements
The Muvipix.com Guide to DVD Architect
The Muvipix.com Guides to Vegas Movie Studio HD 10 and 11
The Muvipix.com Guide to Vegas Movie Studio 14
The Muvipix.com Guides to Sony Movie Studio 12 and 13
The Muvipix.com Guides to CyberLink PowerDirector 12, 13, 14 and 15
The Muvipix.com Guides to Adobe Premiere Elements 7, 8, 9 ,10 ,11, 12 ,13, 14, 15 and Premiere Elements 2018
The Muvipix.com Guides to Photoshop Elements & Premiere Elements 7, 8 , 9 ,10, 11, 12 ,13, 14, 15 and Photoshop Elements 2018

An Introduction

We created Muvipix.com way back in 2006 as both a community where fellow videomakers from around the world could share ideas and ask questions and as a site where we could provide a library of basic, intermediate and advanced tutorials.

As we were building this library, we found that, once people understood the basics of video editing, there were a number of effects many seemed to want to create.

How do I highlight someone in a crowd?

How do blur someone's face like they do on COPS?

How do I make someone standing in front of a green screen look like he or she is on a distant planet?

How do I make someone look like he or she is flying?

How do I create the effect of a line moving across a map?

How do I make a scrolling title sequence that vanishes off into space like at the beginning of the Star Wars movies?

You'll find step-by-step instructions for creating each of these effects in this book. In fact, you'll find easy step-by-step instructions for creating *50* very cool, oft-requested video and audio effects in this book!

The book, of course, assumes you've got a basic understanding of Premiere Elements. But, just in case, we review the basics in Chapter 1. And, if you need a bit more detailed instructions, we've got a free 8-part Basic Training tutorial series at Muvipix.com. (Just type "Basic training for Premiere Elements" into the home page's product search box.)

Hopefully the tricks in this book (along with dozens of Hot Tips we've thrown in along with way) will guide and inspire you – not just to create the effects we show you, but to discover and great even cooler effects on your own.

And, if you get stuck along the way – or just want to say hello – please drop by our free Muvipix Community Forum. We or one of our other friendly Muvipixers will be more than happy to help you out.

Have fun!

Muvipix.com was created in 2006 as a community and a learning center for videomakers at a variety of levels. Our community includes everyone from amateurs and hobbyists to semi-pros, professionals and even people with broadcast experience. You won't find more knowledgeable, helpful people anywhere else on the Web. I very much encourage you to drop by our forums and say hello. At the very least, you'll make some new friends. And it's rare that there's a question posted that isn't quickly, and enthusiastically, answered.

Our learning center consists of video tutorials, tips and, of course, books. But we also offer a wealth of support in the form of custom-created DVD and BluRay disc menus, motion background videos, licensed music and even stock footage. Much of it is absolutely free – and there's even more available for those who purchase one of our affordable site subscriptions.

Our goal has always been to help people get up to speed making great videos and, once they're there, to provide them with the inspiration and means to get better and better at doing so.

Why? Because we know making movies and taking great pictures is a heck of a lot of fun – and we want to share that fun with everyone!

Our books, then, are a manifestation of that goal. And my hope for you is that this book helps *you* get up to speed. I think you'll find that, once you learn the basics, making movies on your home computer is a lot more fun than you ever imagined! And you may even amaze yourself with the results in the process.

Thanks for supporting Muvipix.com, and happy moviemaking!

Steve
http://Muvipix.com

Cool Tricks & Hot Tips for Adobe Premiere Elements 2018

Cool Tricks

Chapter 5

Cool Keyframing Tricks 57
Effects that move and change

Chapter 6

Cool Transition Tricks 69
Interesting ways to get from one clip to another

Chapter 7

Cool Video Grid Tricks 81
Tricks with tracks

Chapter 8

Cool Tricks with Time................................97
Speeding things up and slowing things down

Chapter 9

Cool Track Matte Tricks 105
Cutting holes through your videos

Chapter 10

Cool Picture-in-Picture Tricks..........................121
Doubling up your videos

Hot Tips

Table of Contents

Chapter 1
Basic Video Editing Moves
An overview of the basic steps of non-linear editing

Every great journey begins with a few simple steps. And, likewise, even the most elaborate video project begins with the same basic moves.

In this chapter, we'll review the basic moves for creating and editing a Premiere Elements project. Because, as you'll see as we continue, even the most advanced effect is really just a series of simple moves – but done with flourish!

No matter what you plan to do with your video and no matter how creatively you plan to do it, the video editing process itself will still fit the same basic structure.

Here's a brief walkthrough of the steps you'll take for creating any video project in Premiere Elements.

1 Gather your media

The assets, or media, you gather to create your movie can come from a variety of sources. It can be video, audio, music, photos or graphics. If you are working in Quick View, any media you gather will go directly to your timeline. If you are working in Expert View, it will go into your **Project Assets** panel.

To import your media into your project, click on the **Add Media** tab on the upper left of the interface.

There are basically three ways to get your media into your project, all accessed by one of the six buttons on the **Add Media** panel (illustrated below).

- **Download your video from a hard drive camcorder, flash based camcorder or other video recording device.**

  Video clips from hard drive and flash drive recording devices, including high-definition AVCHD, 4K and Go Pro camcorders as well as smart phones, are *downloaded* into your Premiere Elements project when you select the **Videos from Cameras & Devices** option. Media can also be downloaded from other sources, including DVDs, using the **DVD Camera or Computer Drive** option. Photos can be added from cameras and other devices by selecting the **Photos from Cameras or Devices** option.

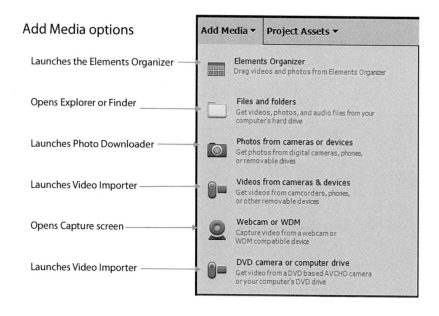

Add Media options

Launches the Elements Organizer —— Elements Organizer
Drag videos and photos from Elements Organizer

Opens Explorer or Finder —— Files and folders
Get videos, photos, and audio files from your computer's hard drive

Launches Photo Downloader —— Photos from cameras or devices
Get photos from digital cameras, phones, or removable drives

Launches Video Importer —— Videos from cameras & devices
Get videos from camcorders, phones, or other removable devices

Opens Capture screen —— Webcam or WDM
Capture video from a webcam or WDM compatible device

Launches Video Importer —— DVD camera or computer drive
Get video from a DVD based AVCHD camera or your computer's DVD drive

Video **streamed** from your webcam is captured live through the Premiere Elements Capture workspace.

Video from non-tape-based sources – including hard drive and AVCHD camcorders, DVDs and smartphones – is **downloaded** into your Premiere Elements project by the Video Importer, while still photos are downloaded from your digital camera or phone by the Photo Downloader.

When you select the option to Add Media from the Organizer, you can locate the photos, video and audio files already on your computer using the Organizer's management tools and **import** it into your project.

- **Stream, or capture, your video into your project.**

  If you've got a **Webcam or other WDM** (Windows Device Model) video or audio device attached to your computer, you can use Premiere Elements to *capture* the live video directly into your Premiere Elements video project.

  Premiere Elements 2018 does not include tools for capturing tape-based video, including video from HDV and miniDV camcorders. However, video from digital tape camcorders *can* be captured over an IEEE-1394 (FireWire) connection as Premiere Elements-compatible video data using various third-party software and then added to your Premiere Elements project.

  We recommend you use WinDV to capture from a miniDV camcorder. To capture from an HDV camcorder we recommend you can use HDV Split. Both are free downloads and capture your digital tape-based video via a FireWire connection. On a Mac, our favorite tape capture program is Lifeflix, available from the App Store.

- **Browse to gather and import media files that are located on your computer's hard drive(s).**

  When you click the **PC Files and Folders** button under **Add Media**, Windows Explorer or the Mac OSX Finder will open, allowing you to *import* video, stills, graphics or music files already on your computer's hard drive. The **Elements Organizer** is a companion file management program that can be used to manage and search media files on your computer.

3

To add a clip to your timeline in Expert View, simply drag it from the Project Assets panel.

As you add clips tp the middle of a project, the other clips will "ripple", or move to the right.

To override the ripple effect (as when you're adding music or a video clip to a parallel track) hold down the Ctrl key as you add the clip (or the Command key on a Mac).

Zoom in or out on the timeline by pressing + or - or using the Zoom slider.

2   Assemble the clips on your timeline

Once you've imported your media clips into a project, you can begin the process of assembling your movie. If you are working in Quick View, any media you add to your project will be loaded directly to your timeline. If you are working in Expert View, the clips will be added to your **Project Assets** panel. Editing this video is as simple as dragging these clips from this panel to your timeline.

Once you add your files to your timeline, you'll have a number of options:

- Trim your clips. Trimming means removing footage from either the beginning or the end of a clip. To trim a clip, click to select the clip on your timeline and then drag in from either its beginning or end, as in the illustration on the following page.

- Split your clips. Splitting means slicing through your clips so that you can remove footage from the middle or delete a sliced-off segment completely. To split a clip, position the **CTI** (playhead) over your clip at the point at which you'd like the slice to occur and then click on the scissors icon on **CTI**.

- Place your clip on an upper video or audio track. An important feature of editing in Expert View is the ability to place your video or audio on tracks other than **Video 1** and **Audio 1**.

The use of multiple tracks of video is, in fact, key to the creation of many of the more advanced video effects, including **Chroma Key** and **Videomerge**, and to creating advanced video effects like *Cool Trick 23, Create a "Brady Bunch" Video Grid.*

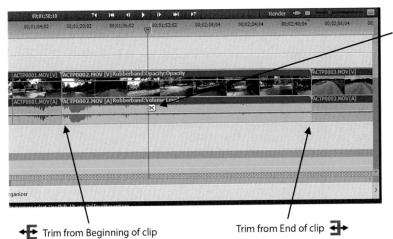

To slice a clip in two, click the scissors icon on the CTI playhead.

If a clip is selected on the timeline, only that clip will be split at the position of the CTI; If no clips are selected, all clips on every track on the timeline will be split at the position of the CTI.

◄🄴 Trim from Beginning of clip

Trim from End of clip 🄴►

To trim a clip on the timeline, hover your mouse over the beginning or end of a clip until the Trim from Beginning or Trim from End icon appears, then click and drag in or out.

3 Add and adjust effects

Premiere Elements comes loaded with dozens of video and audio effects as well as hundreds of preset effects for working magic on your movie.

Adding an effect in Premiere Elements is very easy.

1 Click the Effects button.

As illustrated on the next page, the **Effects** button is located on the **Toolbar** along the right side of the program.

This will open the **Effects** panel.

2 Locate an effect.

Go to any category of video or audio effects by clicking the title bar (The bar along the top of the panel) and selecting from the list that appears.

You can also quickly locate any effect by clicking the **Quick Search** magnifying glass button at the top right of the panel and typing in the effect's name.

3 Apply the effect.

To apply an effect, drag it from the **Effects** panel onto a clip on your timeline.

4 Adjust the effect's settings.

Once you've applied your effect, you may or may not see an immediate change in your video clip. To intensify or fine tune your effect, ensure the clip is selected on your timeline, then open the **Applied Effects** panel by clicking its button on the **Toolbar**.

The **Applied Effects** panel is a tremendously powerful workspace. Not only can you use it to change the settings for individual effects, but it also serves as the main workspace for creating and adjusting **keyframes**, Premiere Elements' system for creating animations, motion paths and effects that change over the course of the clip's playback.

On the **Applied Effects** panel, locate your effect's listing, then click on it to open the effect's settings.

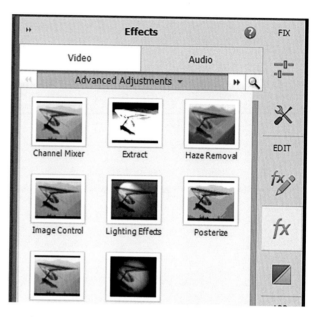

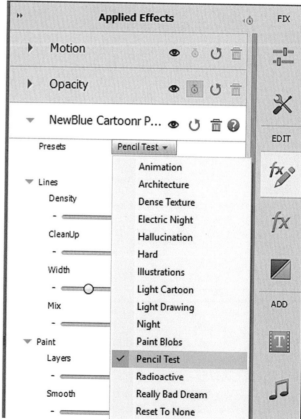

Effects that have been added to a clip appear in that clip's Applied Effects panel, where they can be adjusted and customized.

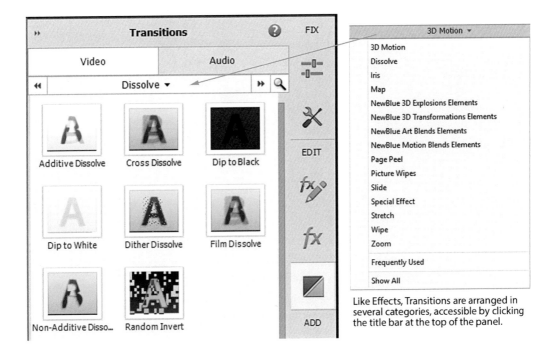

Like Effects, Transitions are arranged in several categories, accessible by clicking the title bar at the top of the panel.

4 Add and adjust transitions

Transitions are the effects or animations that take your movie from one clip to another. Some are gentle and nearly invisible – others are showy and draw attention to themselves. Most transitions are added to your timeline and adjusted similarly to effects:

1 Click on the Transitions button on the Toolbar.

The **Transitions** panel will open.

2 Locate a transition.

Select any category of video or audio effects by clicking the title bar (The bar along the top of the panel) and selecting from the pop-up list that appears.

You can also quickly locate any effect by clicking the **Quick Search** magnifying glass button at the top right of the panel and typing in the transition's name.

3 Apply the transition.

Apply a transition by dragging it from the **Transitions** panel onto the intersection of two clips on your timeline.

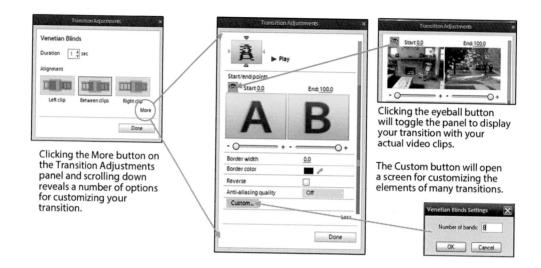

Clicking the More button on the Transition Adjustments panel and scrolling down reveals a number of options for customizing your transition.

Clicking the eyeball button will toggle the panel to display your transition with your actual video clips.

The Custom button will open a screen for customizing the elements of many transitions.

4   Customize your transition.

Nearly all transitions include a number of properties that can be customized, depending on the nature of the transition. Virtually all transitions include options for designating where the transition centers, the duration of the transition and for optionally setting the transition to reverse its movement (i.e., wiping from right to left rather than left to right).

5 Add titles

Titles are text, and sometimes graphics, placed over your clips to provide additional visual information for your video story. Once you've selected a title template, you'll create and customize your titles in Premiere Elements' **Title Adjustments** workspace.

To add a title or text to your movie:

1   Click the Titles & Text button on the Toolbar.

The **Titles & Text** panel will open.

As with **Effects** and **Transitions**, the panel has several categories of title templates. Among these are text-only stationary titles, titles with graphics and rolling and animated titles. In addition to standard title templates, the library includes a collection of **Motion Titles** – animated tiles with several customizable elements.

2   Add the title to your timeline.

Drag the title from the **Titles & Templates** panel to your timeline. The **Title Adjustments** workspace will automatically open.

3   Customize your title's text.

Type your custom text over the placeholder text.

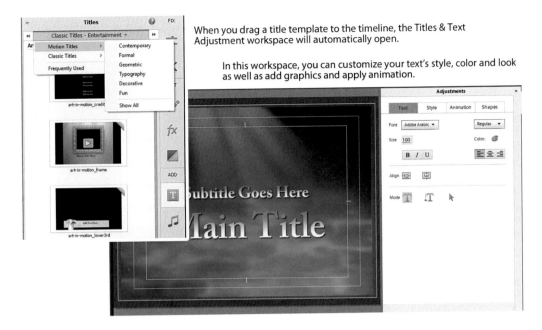

When you drag a title template to the timeline, the Titles & Text Adjustment workspace will automatically open.

In this workspace, you can customize your text's style, color and look as well as add graphics and apply animation.

With your text block selected, you can customize the text's attributes – including the font, size, style and alignment. You can also apply a style to your selected text by clicking on one of the **Text Styles** listed on the panel.

4   Customize your title's look and animation.

The **Title Adjustments** workspace has tools for customizing the look and style of your text, adding and placing graphics and adding very cool text animations. You can also create rolling and crawling titles.

When you want to return to the regular editing workspace, click on the timeline.

Need some Basic Training?

Want some free hands-on training with the basics of Premiere Elements?

Check out my free tutorial series **Basic Training with Premiere Elements** at Muvipix.com.

This simple, eight-part series will show you how to set up a project, how to import media into it, basic editing moves, adding transitions and effects, how to create titles, how to add and customize your DVD and BluRay disc menu navigation markers and how to export your finished video. And did I mention that it's free?

To see the series, just go to http://Muvipix.com and type "Premiere Elements Basic Training" in the product search box. And while you're there, why not drop by the Community forum and say hi! We'd love to have you become a part of our growing city. Happy moviemaking!

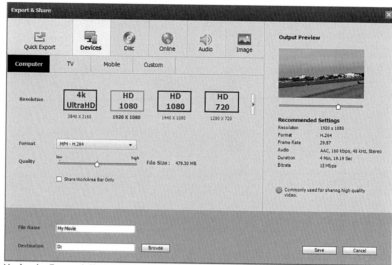

Under the Export & Share tab, you'll find several options for outputting your movie.

6   Export & Share your movie

When you're happy with the movie you've created, you'll find a number of options for publishing and sharing it, as we discuss in **Chapter 21**. We'll show you how to output your movie to:

- **Devices.** The program will save your finished project as an AVI file, MPEG, QuickTime (MOV) file, AVCHD video, Windows Media (WMV) file or an audio file on your computer's hard drive. Once the output is complete, you can then use these files any number of ways, including posting them online or using them as segments in a larger video project.

- **Disc.** Built into Premiere Elements are tools for creating menus and scene markers so you can produce great-looking DVDs.

- **Online.** The program comes complete with tools for loading your finished video to a social media site like YouTube, Vimeo or Facebook.

- **Audio** or **Image.** Premiere Elements also includes tools for outputting an audio file or a still photo from your movie.

And that's basically it!

You gather your assets; you assemble them on your timeline; you add effects, transitions and titles; then you share your masterpiece with the world.

But between the lines of this simplicity are the countless variations that can elevate your movie project from the realm of a basic structure to something truly amazing!

This book is about 50 of them.

Chapter 2
Cool Basic Effects
Working with what's there

There are many cool things you can do with your movie just using the basic set of effects included with Premiere Elements.

Virtually every effect includes internal settings for customizing its look and functionality – and, once you get comfortable changing these settings, you'll be amazed how many imaginative effects you can create!

Premiere Elements includes over 80 video effects and nearly 20 audio effects, virtually all of which are customizable to some extent.

Additionally, the program includes over 250 preset effects – ready-made effects to which custom settings or animations have already been applied.

To access the program's library of video and audio, click on the **Effects** button on the **Toolbar** that runs along the bottom of the program.

As you can see in the illustration on the opposite page, these effects are arranged in categories under **Video** and **Audio** tabs. Any category can be accessed directly by clicking on the **Category** bar at the top of the panel. You can go directly to any effect by clicking the magnifying glass in the upper right of the panel and typing the name of the effect into the **Quick Search** box that appears (as illustrated in the *Hot Tip* on page 14).

Once you've applied an effect, you can customize it and change its properties and settings on the clip's **Applied Effects** panel. The **Applied Effects** panel is also the principal workspace for **keyframing**, the process of animating your effects and creating motion paths for your photos. As you work through this book, you'll become very familiar with the tools in this very workspace.

Effects

Here is a brief overview of the Premiere Elements video effects set.

Advanced Adjustments. The **Advanced Adjustments** effects work primarily with color. These are the effects you'll use if you want to change or correct color in your clip.

Additionally, **Lighting Effects** imposes a spotlight-like effect on your clip. We put it to work in *Cool Trick 2*.

Blur Sharpen. These effects soften or sharpen your picture.

HOT TIP
The Mac version has a limited set of effects

The Mac version of Premiere Elements omits some of the effects available in the PC version. The following **video effects** not included in the Mac version are:

Blur & Sharpen: Anti-Alias, Ghosting

Distort: Bend, Lens Distortion

Image Control: Color Pass, Color Replace

Keying: Blue Screen Key, Green Screen Key, Chroma Key, RGB Difference Key

Transform: Camera View, Clip, Horizontal Hold, Vertical Hold

The following **audio effects** are not included in the Mac version:

Denoiser, Dynamics, Pitch Shifter, Reverb

To apply an effect to a clip on your timeline, simply drag it onto the clip from the Effects panel.

Categories can be brpwsed by clicking on the Category Title Bar at the top of the panel or by navigating from category to category clicking the arrows.

The Quick Search tool will locate any effect. (See the sidebar on page 14.)

Preview the animation for any Preset effect by clicking on its thumbnail.

After an effect is applied, it can be adjusted on the Applied Effects panel.

The Effects panel is launched by clicking the Effects button.

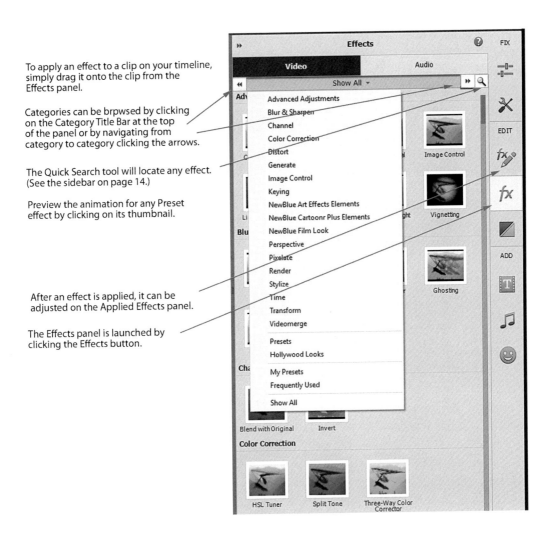

The **Ghosting** effects leaves a very cool trail behind objects that are moving in your clip.

Channel. Invert, the single **Channel** effect, turns your video's picture into its negative.

Color Correction. The effects in this set – **HSL Tuner, Split Tone** and the **Three-Way Color Corrector** – are advanced tools for enhancing and correcting the color in your video.

Distort. The **Distort** effects warp, twist and/or bend your video image. The **Corner Pin** effect in this category helps us create Star Wars-style titles in *Cool Trick 48*.

Generate. The **Lens Flare** effect in this category adds a bright, white flare to a spot on your video picture, as if a light is being shone back at the camcorder. We use it to create a shooting star in our *Cool Trick 5*.

Image Control. Among this set are tools for tinting, replacing and even removing the color completely from your video.

Keying. Keying effects remove or make transparent a portion of your video's picture.

A powerful tool in this category is the **Chroma Key** effect, which we put to good use in *Cool Tricks 36, 39, 40* and *41*. Because **Chroma Key** is not included in the Mac version of Premiere Elements, Mac users will use the **Videomerge** effect instead.

Others, like the **Garbage Mattes**, create transparent areas in a clip that can be shaped with user-defined corner handles. We'll show you a great fun way to use this effect in *Cool Trick 38*.

And the **Track Matte** effect in this category is so powerful, we dedicate all of **Chapter 9**'s *Cool Tricks* to it!

NewBlue Art Effects, NewBlue Film Look. These effects categories include high-level image effects created by NewBlue, one of the world's top video effects companies.

One of the most popular of these is the **Old Film** effect, a highly customizable effect which makes your video look like a damaged, worn, old movie. You can see it at work in *Cool Trick 14*.

NewBlue Cartoonr Plus Elements. This effect makes your videos look cartoon-like. We put it to work in *Cool Trick 4*.

Perspective. These effects can be used to make your video image look as if it is floating or rotating into space. We use this category's **Basic 3D** effect in *Cool Trick 22*.

HOT TIP
A quick way to locate an effect

The **Quick Search** tool on the **Effects** panel is a way to quickly locate any effect.

To use this tool, just click on the magnifying glass in the upper right of the panel. This will open a search box.

Type the name of the effect in this box and, as you type, Premiere Elements will locate the effect in "real time." That means, by the time you type "cro", the program will have already located for you the **Crop** effect.

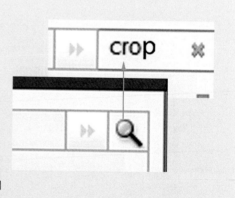

Click the **X** at the right end of the **Quick Search** box to turn off the search filter and reset the panel to **Show All**.

Pixelate. The **Facet** effect in this category reduces your video picture to a group of large color blocks.

Render. The **Lightning** effect is great fun, although it takes a lot of computer power to create and customize it!

The **Ramp** effect fades your video out across the screen in a gradiated pattern. We put it to use in *Cool Trick 50.*

Stylize. The effects in this category, as the category name implies, can be used to create a highly stylized video. We'll use it to blur a face as on TV's *COPS* in *Cool Trick 30.*

Time. Effects in this category change how your video displays motion by reducing or affecting the look of the frame rate.

Note that this is *not* the place to go if you want to slow down or speed up a clip. To create that effect, you'll use either the **Time Stretch** effect (which we use in *Cool Trick 25*) or the Time Remapping tool (which we use in *Cool Trick 26.*

Transform. A real hodgepodge of effects, this category includes some stylized effects, some 3D transformations and, for some reason, **Clip** and **Crop**, two effects for trimming off the sides of your video picture.

For the record, **Clip** trims away the sides of your video and replaces them with color while **Crop** trims away the sides and replaces them with transparency – a significant difference, if you're using your cropped clip on an upper video track with another clip on a track below it. We use the **Crop** tool to create some very cool map effects in *Cool Tricks 45, 46* and *47.*

Videomerge. This effect is essentially a more automatic version of the **Chroma Key** effect. When applied to a clip, it removes what it interprets to be the background in a single step. You can see it work in *Cool Trick 37.*

Audio Effects. We'll take a closer look at these effects in **Chapter 3.**

Presets. A collection of nearly 300 pre-created effects for your movie, many of them animated. We'll show you an innovative use for some of them in *Cool Trick 17.*

Hollywood Looks. Hollywood Looks are adjustments to your video's tints and saturations that can change the entire tone of your movie with a single click. Included are looks for shifting skins tones to blue, deadening the colors for a horror film effect, shifting tints to make your video look like an old movie, and a de-saturator for giving your movie a film noir look.

My Presets, a folder for storing your own custom-created effects and animations.

Create a "Fish Eye" Look

1. Click the Effects button on the Toolbar and locate the Spherize effect in the Distort category.

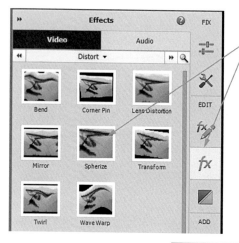

2. Drag the effect onto the clip.

3. With the clip selected, open the Applied Effects panel and click on the Spherize effect.

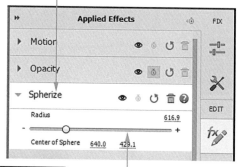

4. Adjust the Radius slider so that the entire video frame is included in the sphere – about 350-400 pixels on a standard definition video or 600-650 on a high-def clip.

COOL TRICK

1 Create a "Fish Eye" Look

Effects can be used to create a mood in your video. The "Fish Eye" effect has often been used to create a feeling of paranoia, making it look like the world has suddenly become a strange place. It is also often used to give the feeling that the person whose point-of-view it's providing is under the influence of a drug or is suffering hallucinations.

Usually, this effect is accomplished through the use of a special "fish eye" lens. A "fish eye" is an extremely wide angle lens that distorts the image so that what's toward the center of the video frame seems unnaturally close while things around the edge seem unnaturally far away. And, as the camera pans around, the imagery seems to curve strangely as if wrapped around a ball. Think of the effect of looking through a peephole in a hotel room door or seeing a reflection in a round hubcap or Christmas tree ornament.

Although movies and video are often shot through a "fish eye" lens to create this effect, you can also add or exaggerate the effect in post-production.

1   **Locate the Spherize effect**

Click the **Effects** button on the **Toolbar.**

The **Spherize** effect is located in the **Distort** category of **Video Effects.**

2   **Apply the Spherize effect**

Drag the effect from the **Effects** panel onto a clip on your timeline.

You won't likely see a big change in your clip at first.

3   **Open the clip's Applied Effects panel**

With the clip selected on the timeline, click the **Applied Effects** button on the right side of the program's interface.

4   **Adjust the Lens Distortion effect for your clip**

Click on the listing for the **Spherize** effect on the Applied Effects panel to open the effect's settings.

Move the **Radius** slider until your entire video frame, as displayed in the **Monitor**, is spherized (as illustrated on the previous page). This will likely be at a **Radius** setting of between 350 and 450 pixels for standard definition video – though it could be twice that for high-def.

Your "fish eye" effect will be most effective when there is some motion in your video frame and when objects or people are very close to the camera, emphasizing the distortion.

COOL TRICK

2 Spotlight an Area in Your Video

Sometimes you want to isolate a person or thing in your video. Maybe you want to point out a person in a crowd shot or highlight a sentence or word on a page of text.

One way to do this is to **spotlight** the person or thing you want to highlight. In this *Cool Trick*, we'll use **Lighting Effects** to dim or darken the imagery around our focal point, as if the lights have gone down and the person or thing we want to direct your audience's attention to is the only thing lit (as illustrated on the following page).

Spotlight an Area of Your Video

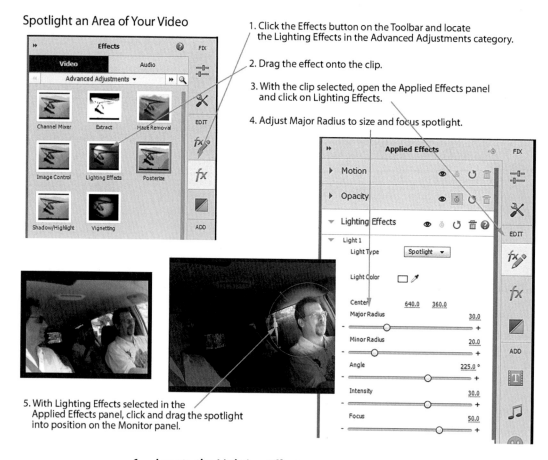

1. Click the Effects button on the Toolbar and locate the Lighting Effects in the Advanced Adjustments category.

2. Drag the effect onto the clip.

3. With the clip selected, open the Applied Effects panel and click on Lighting Effects.

4. Adjust Major Radius to size and focus spotlight.

5. With Lighting Effects selected in the Applied Effects panel, click and drag the spotlight into position on the Monitor panel.

1 Locate the Lighting Effects

Click the **Effects** button on the **Toolbar.**

The **Lighting Effects** are located in the **Advanced Adjustments** category of **Video Effects.**

2 Apply the Lighting Effects

Drag the effect from the **Effects** panel onto a clip on your timeline.

In the **Monitor,** your video image will appear to dim, except for a spotlit area in the middle of the frame.

3 Open the clip's Applied Effects panel

With the clip selected on the timeline, click the **Applied Effects** button on the right side of the program's interface.

Click on the listing for the **Lighting Effects** on the **Applied Effects** panel to open the effect's settings.

By default, this effect includes a basic spotlight – although, as you can see, you can create as many as five lights for your video at once.

4   Adjust the spotlight

Click the little triangle to the left of **Light 1** to open its settings.

The **Major Radius** is the width of the spotlit area itself. Raise or lower the slider to create the size of highlight you'd like to create.

The **Minor Radius** controls how evenly the light spreads. You'll likely want to keep it the same as the **Major Radius** for this particular effect.

Adjust the **Intensity** to a natural level, around 30-35%.

5   Position the spotlight

Finally, we'll want to position the spot so that it's over the person or thing we want to highlight.

The **Center** of the spotlight is indicated numerically, just above the sliders. These numbers indicate the distance, measured in pixels, the center of the spotlight is from the upper left corner of the video frame.

An NTSC video frame is 720x480 pixels, so a spotlight in the center of the frame will be at 360 240. A high-definition video frame is 1920x1080 pixels; a spotlight in its center would be at 960 540.

We could type in the numbers for our new position manually or even click and drag to scrub across the numbers and roll their values up and down – but there's a more intuitive way to position your spotlight.

Click on the **Lighting Effects** listing in the **Applied Effects** panel. The spotlight's position on your **Monitor** will appear as a center point and circle with four "corner handles" around the circle's circumference.

HOT TIP
A more intuitive way to change effects settings

Often the easiest way to change an effect's position or setting is to drag the effect into position or resize it right on the **Monitor** panel. To change, for instance, a clip's size, click on the **Motion** effect's listing in the **Applied Effects** panel (**Scale** is **Motion** setting) and then drag the clip larger or smaller by its corner handles on the **Monitor** panel.

Effects like **Crop** and **Clip** as well as the positions of the lights in **Lighting Effects** can likewise be most intuitively sized or positioned by clicking to select the effect's listing the **Applied Effects** panel and then manipulating the clip in the **Monitor** panel.

As you hover your mouse over the center of this circle, a small icon of a light bulb will appear with the number "1" next to it. This indicates that you are in position to select and move this spotlight's location.

Click on this center point in the circle and drag the spotlight to the position in your video frame that you'd like it to highlight.

As with nearly all effects adjusted in the **Applied Effects** panel, the characteristics of this spotlight, including its position, can be **keyframed** so that it follows the movement of a person or object around you video frame.

Instructions on how to keyframe this type of motion can be found in my book *The Muvipix.com Guide to Premiere Elements*. We also have a free "Basic Keyframing" tutorial at Muvipix.com.

Another effect that can be used to isolate a person or object in your video frame is the **Track Matte**. We show you how to do that in *Cool Trick 29, Isolate a Person in a Crowd*.

COOL TRICK

3 Make Your Video Roll Like It's On a Broken TV

This effect makes your video look like it's being show on a broken TV. It really doesn't have too many other applications beyond that.

It's a very simple trick – but still kind of fun. It's a great one to use in combination with *Cool Trick 35, Make Your Video Look Like It's on TV* to give the illusion that some poor soul is trying to watch a TV on the fritz.

That's right: Effects can be combined and piled onto each other – creating an even cooler effect than either effect would on its own.

1   Locate the Horizontal Hold effect

Click the **Effects** button on the **Toolbar.**

The **Horizontal Hold** effect is located in the **Transform** category of **Video Effects**.

2   Apply Horizontal Hold to your clip

Drag the effect from the **Effects** panel onto a clip on your timeline.

In the **Monitor,** your video image will distort and tilt slightly to the left.

Make Your Video Roll Like it's on a Broken TV

1. Click the Effects button on the Tooolbar and locate the Horizontal Hold effect in the Transform category.

2. Drag the effect onto the clip.

3. Locate and apply the Vertical Hold effect also.

4. Open the clip's Applied Effects panel and click on the Horizontal Hold effects to open its settings.

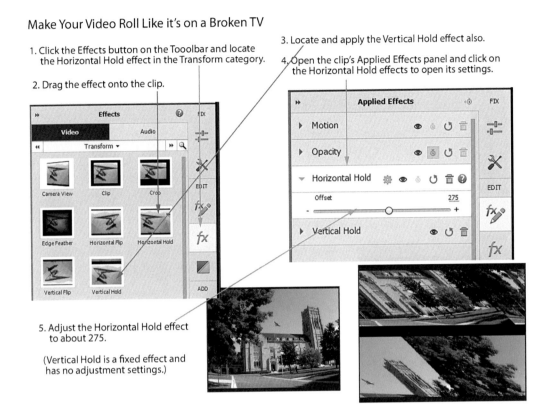

5. Adjust the Horizontal Hold effect to about 275.

(Vertical Hold is a fixed effect and has no adjustment settings.)

3   Locate and apply the Vertical Hold effect

The **Vertical Roll** effect is also located in the **Transform** category of **Video Effects**.

Drag the effect from the **Effects** panel onto a clip on your timeline.

4   Open the clip's Applied Effects panel

With the clip selected on the timeline, click the **Applied Effects** button on the right side of the program's interface.

5   Adjust the Horizontal Hold effect

Click on the listing for the **Horizontal Hold** effect on the **Applied Effects** panel to open the effect's settings.

Adjust the **Horizontal Hold** slider to really screw up your picture.

275 is a good setting.

Vertical Hold is a fixed effect and can not be adjusted.

Because the **Vertical Hold** effect is a fixed effect, you can't keyframe this special effect. At least not the **Vertical Hold** aspect of it. But, if you'd like to add some variation to this effect – making it look like the picture is wavering in and out, there's a simple way to do it.

Position the **CTI** (the playhead) a few seconds into your clip and click on the little scissors icon that appears (the **Split Tool**) when you hover your mouse over the playhead (as illustrated on page 5). Move the **CTI** a little further to the right and click the **Split Tool** again.

The Split Tool

Now click on the segment of the clip you've isolated between your splits and open the **Applied Effects** panel. In the **Applied Effects** panel, click on the little trashcan icon to the right of the listings for **Horizontal Hold** and **Vertical Hold** effects to remove them.

Now, when you play your clip, your video will look screwed up – then briefly appear clear, then go back to being screwed up.

This trick – splitting up your clip to isolate segments and apply effects to only portions of your larger clip – is a great way to vary an effect's level without keyframing. And it's particularly effective in situations, like this, in which keyframing isn't available.

COOL TRICK

4 "Cartoon" Your Video

This is a fun special effect and a real attention getter. And thanks to its designers at NewBlue, its cool effects are as easy to create as they are dazzling!

The **Cartoonr Plus** effect works by doing two things: "posterizing" the color in your video so that its smooth, natural color is reduced to a few basic colors, and blackening or thickening breaks between colors to give the impression that its lines were drawn with a black ink pen.

It's actually a pretty complicated effect. If you open the effect in the **Applied Effects** panel, you'll see that there are 13 different sliders for fine-tuning the **Line** and **Paint** properties!

But you needn't bother with those adjustments, except for a little fine tuning here and there because the effect also comes loaded with an easy-to-use library of **presets** for achieving a number of variations on the effect.

1   **Locate the NewBlue Cartoonr Plus effect**

Click the **Effects** button on the **Toolbar**.

The **NewBlue Cartoonr Plus** effect is located in the **NewBlue Art Effects Cartoonr Plus Elements** category of **Video Effects**.

"Cartoon" Your Video

1. Locate the NewBlue Cartoonr Plus effect in the NewBlue Cartoonr Plus Elements category.

2. Apply the Cartoonr Plus effect to a clip.

3. Open the clip's Applied Effects.

4. Select an option from the Preset menu— or make fine tuning adjustments to Paint and Lines settings.

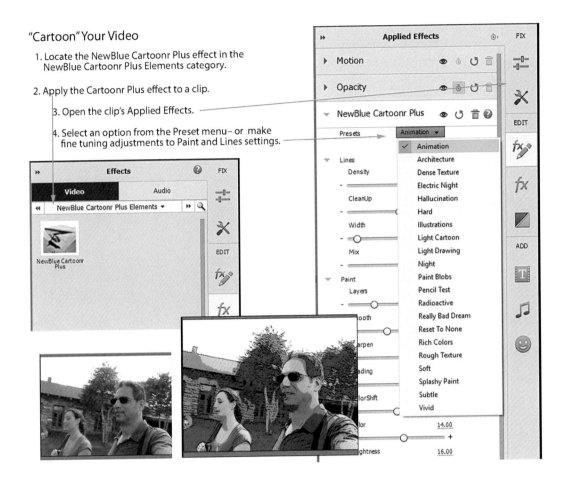

2 Apply the Cartoonr effect

Drag the effect from the **Effects** panel onto a clip on your timeline.

In the **Monitor**, your video image will appear with a reduced number of colors and the shadows and darker spots appearing as if drawn by a pen.

This is the default setting for the **Cartoonr** effect, the **Animation** preset. But it's by no means the only cartoon look this effect is capable of producing.

3 Open the clip's Applied Effects

With the clip selected on the timeline, click the **Applied Effects** button on the right side of the program's interface.

4 Apply a Cartoonr Plus preset

Click on the **NewBlue Cartoonr Plus** listing on the **Applied Effects** panel to open the effect's properties and settings.

The **Presets** drop-down menu is located at the center top of the **NewBlue Cartoonr Plus** effect's settings, as illustrated on the previous page. Click on the drop-down to open the **Preset** menu.

The **Cartoonr** effect has 21 presets, ranging from the look of an animated cartoon to a psychedelic **Hallucination** to a creepy **Night** painting to a **Pencil Test** line drawing. Test driving a preset is as simple as selecting it from the list. Don't like it? Try another.

Particularly as you work with audio effects (as we will in the next chapter), selecting from a menu of presets can greatly simplify the process of customizing an effect.

COOL TRICK
5 Add a Shooting Star to Your Video

Often you'll use an effect exactly as it's designed to be used. And, with Premiere Elements' effects collection, doing that alone can keep you pretty busy. But every once in a while it's fun to push the envelope a little. To use a stock effect in a way that creates a whole new effect.

The shooting star effect falls into that category. We'll be using the **Lens Flare** effect to create our shooting star – and then we'll animate it with keyframed motion to it so that our fireball seems to fly across the sky.

This combination of keyframing and the innovative use of an existing effect opens up all kinds of possibilities for your own custom special effects.

For best results with this effect, you'll need a shot of city skyline (as in my illustration) or a distant horizon with lots of sky in the picture. With keyframing, you can animate the effect to match any camera movements – but you'll make it much easier on yourself if your shot is also relatively stationary, with little or no camera movement.

1 **Locate the Lens Flare effect**

Click the **Effects** button on the program's **Toolbar.**

The **Lens Flare** effect is located in the **Generate** category of **Video Effects.**

2 **Apply the Lens Flare effect**

Drag the effect from the **Effects** panel onto a clip on your timeline.

The **Lens Flare** effect creates the illusion that a light is shining back at the camera. For our effect, we'll adjust this flare so that it looks less like a reflected light and more like a fiery ball in the sky.

Add a Shooting Star to Your Video (pt. 1)

1. Locate the Lens Flare effect in the Generate category.

2. Drag the effect onto your clip.

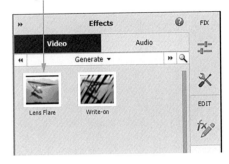

3. With the clip selected, open the Applied Effects panel by clicking the button on the right side of the program's interface.

4. Select the 35mm Prime Lens Type preset.

5. Set Flare Brightness to 70%.

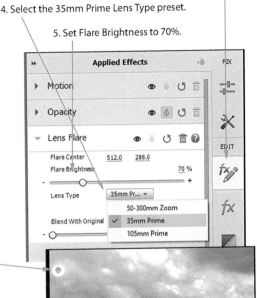

6. With Lens Flare selected in the Applied Effects panel, drag the Flare Center (crosshairs) on Monitor to upper left of frame.

3 Open the clip's Applied Effects

With the clip selected on the timeline, click the **Applied Effects** button on the right side of the program's interface.

4 Select a Lens Flare Lens Type effect

Click on the listing for the **Lens Flare** effect on the **Applied Effects** panel to open its properties and settings.

As you can see, there are several ways to adjust the effect's look and intensity.

The **Lens Type** drop-down menu allows you to select between three different types of light patterns:

The **50-300mm Zoom** light has reddish edges and, at some settings, looks like it's reflecting off your cameras inner lenses with rings of light and other highlights.

The **105mm Prime** is a wider, whiter light.

Use the **35mm Prime** setting, which combines characteristics of the other two and gives us a very bright, focused flare.

5   **Set the Flare Brightness effect**

Use the slider to adjust the **Flare Brightness**. At about 70%, my **Lens Flare** looks almost like the sun shining through the clouds.

6   **Set the initial Flare Center**

We want to position the **Lens Flare Center** in an upper left area of the video frame, about where you'd like it to make its first appearance. (We'll fine tune this position later so that the flare actually enters from outside the frame.)

Although we could adjust the **Flare Center** position by typing in pixel coordinates next to the **Flare Center** listing, the easiest and most intuitive way to adjust this position is to drag the flare into position on the **Monitor** panel.

Click to select the **Lens Flare** effect in the **Applied Effects** panel. When this effect is selected, the **Flare Center** will appear in your **Monitor** panel as crosshairs. Click and drag on the crosshairs to position your **Flare Center**.

7   **Begin a keyframing session**

Keyframing is the method of creating animations or variable effects in Premiere Elements. Using it is as simple as creating sets of keyframing points (representing various effect's settings or positions) and then letting Premiere Elements create the animation between these points.

We'll be using keyframing here to create the movement of the **Lens Flare** across the sky.

To begin a keyframing session, click the **Show Keyframe Controls** button (the stopwatch) on the upper right of the **Applied Effects** panel (as illustrated on the facing page). This will open a mini-timeline in the **Applied Effects** panel representing the duration of the clip.

Position the **CTI** (playhead) on this mini-timeline to the beginning of the clip (or the point at which you want your shooting star to enter your video frame). Then click the **Animation Toggle** (the little stopwatch icon) to the right of the **Lens Flare** effect listing in the **Applied Effects** panel.

A column of little diamond **keyframe** points will appear at the position of the **CTI**, as illustrated.

Add a Shooting Star to Your Video (pt. 2)

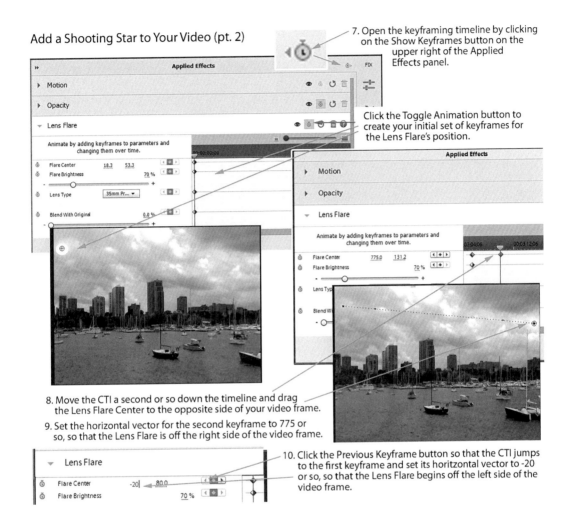

7. Open the keyframing timeline by clicking on the Show Keyframes button on the upper right of the Applied Effects panel.

Click the Toggle Animation button to create your initial set of keyframes for the Lens Flare's position.

8. Move the CTI a second or so down the timeline and drag the Lens Flare Center to the opposite side of your video frame.

9. Set the horizontal vector for the second keyframe to 775 or so, so that the Lens Flare is off the right side of the video frame.

10. Click the Previous Keyframe button so that the CTI jumps to the first keyframe and set its horitzontal vector to -20 or so, so that the Lens Flare begins off the left side of the video frame.

8   Create a second keyframe

Move the **CTI playhead** a second or two to the right. (To make it look like this shooting star is flying across your screen, you'll want to keep its appearance short.)

The **Lens Flare** listing should still be highlighted in the **Applied Effects** panel and the **Flare Center** should still appear as a set of crosshairs on your **Monitor** panel. Click and drag the **Flare Center** crosshairs across the video frame, down slightly and to the right, positioning them as close to the right edge of the frame as you can drag it.

A new keyframe point will automatically appear at your **CTI's** position, representing the effect's new position.

9   Fine tune the second keyframe

Without moving the **CTI**, click on the first number (the horizontal vector) after the **Flare Center** listing in the **Applied Effects** panel and add 60-100 pixels to it (so that it is set to around 775). This will position your **Lens Flare** off the right side of your video frame.

Because high-definition video is 1920x1080 pixels, if you are working in high-definition, your off-screen horizontal vector button will be more like 1950.

Since you have not moved the **CTI**, these new settings will automatically be applied to your existing keyframe.

10   Fine tune the first keyframe

Click on the **Previous Keyframe** button to the right of the **Flare Center** listing in the **Applied Effects** panel (as in the illustration on the previous page). The **CTI** will jump back to the first **Flare Center** keyframe point.

Because we are right on top of this keyframe, we can make adjustments to the effect and this keyframe's settings will be automatically updated, just as we saw with the keyframe in **Step 9**.

Click on the first number (the horizontal vector) to the right of the **Flare Center** listing in the **Applied Effects** panel and set it to -20 or whatever is necessary to move your **Lens Flare** off the left side of your video frame.

Depending on how fast your computer is, you may want to **Render** this clip (by pressing Enter) before you play it back.

But, when you do play it back, it should appear that a fiery ball is shooting across the sky.

Speeding up a keyframed effect is easy. To do so, return to the clip's **Applied Effects** panel and move the **Flare Center's** keyframe points closer together.

The closer your keyframes are to each other, the faster your animation!

You can add any number of **Lens Flares** to your video clip, each with its own animation, to create the effect of Earth suffering a major meteor storm, as I did in my demo video at Muvipix.com/CoolTricks2018.php.

And, as you can see from my demo video, sound effects really enhance the effect!

Chapter 3

Cool Audio Tricks

Tweaking and playing with sound

Generally, people don't do a lot with their audio. As long as it's loud enough, they usually leave it as is.

But Premiere Elements includes a number of audio effects worth exploring – some of which are great functional tools, while others are just plain fun!

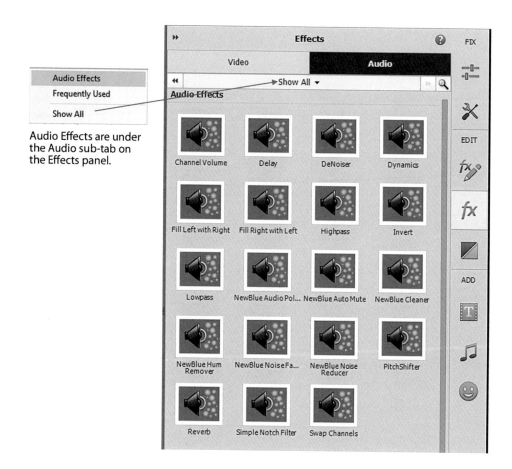

Audio Effects are under the Audio sub-tab on the Effects panel.

The audio effects in Premiere Elements are accessed by clicking on the **Effects** button on the **Toolbar** and then selecting the **Audio** tab.

There are 21 **Audio Effects** in the PC version of Premiere Elements and, as discussed in the sidebar below there are 17 **Audio Effects** in the Mac version.

In addition to these effects, Premiere Elements includes tools for adjusting the **Bass, Treble, Balance** and **Volume** on the **Adjustments** panel, opened by clicking on the **Adjust** button on the right side of the program's interface.

HOT TIP
The Mac version has a limited set of audio effects

The Mac version of Premiere Elements omits some of the audio effects available in the PC version. The audio effects not included in the Mac version are:

Denoiser, Dynamics, PitchShifter, Reverb

Filter effects (**Denoiser, Highpass, Lowpass** and **Notch**) remove certain frequencies of sound. **Dynamics** and **Invert** are audio processors for "sweetening" your movie's sound.

Swap switches the left and right channel's audio.

Fill Right with Left and **Fill Left with Right** are very helpful effects for those times when you have audio on only one of your stereo channels. We show you how to use these great effects in *Cool Trick 8, Make One Audio Channel into Stereo.*

Delay and **Reverb** create echo effects. We show you how to use these effects in *Cool Trick 7, Add an Echo Effect.*

The **Dynamics** and **DeNoiser** effects likewise offer presets for affecting the sound of your audio clip. The **DeNoiser** is primarily designed to clean up tape noise that may have crept into your audio. **Dynamics** provides filters and compressors for limiting audio at certain levels or for evening out louder and quieter sounds. You can use it to reduce unwanted background noise or you can use it to cap high audio levels and avoid overmodulation and distortion.

And just for fun, there's the **PitchShifter**, which changes the pitch of an audio track, usually in very unnatural and often comic ways. We show you this effect in action in *Cool Trick 6, Give Your Characters Funny Voices.*

COOL TRICK

6 Give Your Characters Funny Voices

The **PitchShifter** is a rather extreme audio effect for changing the sounds of your characters' voices.

It really is a just-for-fun tool, as evidenced by the various audio presets the tool offers: **Female Becomes Secret Agent, Cartoon Mouse, Boo!, Sore Throat, Breathless** and **Slightly Detuned.**

(Note that this effect is not available on the Mac version of the program.)

1 Locate the PitchShifter

Click the **Effects** button on the **Toolbar.**

Under the **Audio** tab, click the **Category** bar at the top of the **Effects** panel (as illustrated on page 30) to drop-down the list of effects categories and, from it, select **Audio Effects.**

2 Apply the PitchShifter

Drag the **PitchShifter** effect from the **Effects** panel onto an audio clip on your timeline.

Give Your Characters Funny Voices

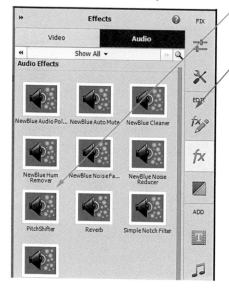

1. Locate the PitchShifter in the Audio Effects.

2. Drag the effect onto a clip's audio.

3. Click the Applied Effects button on the right side of the interface to open the Applied Effects panel.

4. Select a preset from the PitchShifter's preset menu.

5. Test drive and fine tune your effect.

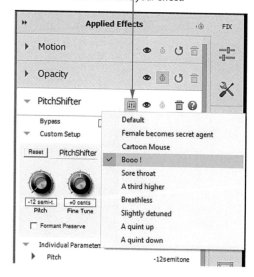

3   Open the clip's Applied Effects panel

With the clip selected on the timeline, click the **Applied Effects** button on the right side of the program's interface.

4   Adjust the PitchShifter settings

Click **PitchShifter** on the **Applied Effects** panel to open the effect's properties and settings.

Although it is possible to manually set the **Individual Parameters** for the **PitchShifter** by tuning the knobs under the effect's **Custom Setup** or by setting the sliders under the effect's **Individual Parameters**, it's usually easiest and most effective to simply select one of the factory **Presets** provided with the effect.

Click the **Preset** button to the right of the **Pitch Shifter** listing and then select a preset from the pop-up menu. **Boo!** for instance.

5   Test drive your effect preset

Play the clip on your timeline.

To replace one **PitchShifter** setting with another, simply select a different preset from the pop-up menu.

HOT TIP
Applying an effect to a segment of a clip

If you'd like to apply an effect to one segment of a clip without affecting another segment of the same clip – say you want to apply the **PitchShifter** to the voice of one person in a clip but not another in the same clip – this can be accomplished in a couple of ways.

You can, of course, **keyframe** the effect, turning the effect on for one segment of the clip and off for another. But there is also a quick-and-dirty method.

To apply an effect to some segments of a clip without affecting other segments of the same clip, position the **CTI** (playhead) and click **Split Clip** (the scissors icon on the **CTI**) to slice your clip into a number of short segments. (These splits will not be heard or seen during playback.) Then apply your effect only to the segments of the clip you want the effect present in – or apply a different effect to each segment!

If you open the **Custom Setup** settings for the **PitchShifter** (by clicking on the little triangle on the left side of the **PitchShifter** settings panel), you'll find a pair of knobs representing **Pitch** and **Fine Tune**, respectively (as illustrated on the facing page). As you apply a preset from the pop-up menu, these knobs will automatically jump to their appropriate settings.

As with any effect of this program, you can continue to fine tune the **PitchShifter** even after a preset has been applied. By adjusting these knobs or the **Individual Parameters** sliders, you can create a wide variety of funny and strange vocal effects.

COOL TRICK
7 Add an Echo Effect

Like the **PitchShifter**, the **Reverb**, or echo effect, is an audio effect that does great things right out of the box. And, like the **PitchShifter**, it includes a set of presets that make the effect very easy to customize for any need. (Note that the Mac version does not include this effect. However, the **Delay** effect can be used in its place, as discussed later in this trick.)

1 Locate the Reverb effect

Click the **Effects** button on the **Toolbar**.

Under the **Audio** tab, click the **Category** bar at the top of the **Effects** panel (as illustrated on page 30) to drop-down the list of effects categories and, from it, select **Audio Effects**.

2 Apply the Reverb effect

Drag the effect from the **Effects** panel onto a clip on your timeline.

Add an Echo Effect

1. Locate Reverb in the Audio Effects.

2. Drag the effect onto a clip's audio.

3. Click the Applied Effects button on the right side of the interface to open the Applied Effects panel.

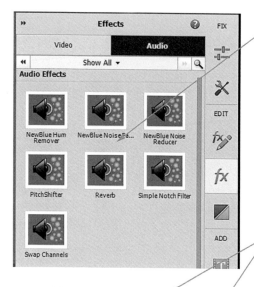

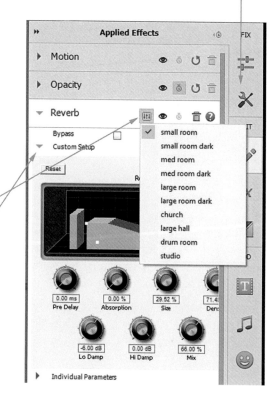

4. Select a preset from the Reverb's pop-up menu.

The Reverb effect can also be fine-tuned by opening the Custom Setup properties and adjusting the individual knobs.

5. Test drive and fine tune your effect.

3 Open the clip's Applied Effects panel

With the clip selected on the timeline, click the **Applied Effects** button on the right side of the program's interface.

4 Adjust the Reverb properties

Click the **Reverb** listing on the **Applied Effects** panel to open the effect's properties and settings.

Although it is possible to manually set parameters, such as the echo delay time, tinniness of the sound and the number of reverberations each sound creates, the easiest way to customize this effect is by selecting one of its intuitively named presets.

Locate and click on the pop-up preset menu to the right of the effect's listing in the **Applied Effects** panel (as in the illustration). The menu will display a list of presets named for various room sizes and other environmental characteristics.

Select a preset from this menu. **Small Room** for instance.

5   Test drive your effect preset

Play the clip on your timeline.

To replace one **Reverb** setting with another, simply select a different preset from the pop-up menu.

One of my favorite things about **Reverb** is how easily its effect is customized using its very intuitively named presets.

The **Small Room** preset really does sound like a little, echoey room, while the **Church** or **Large Hall** presets bounce the sound around as if it were in a huge, empty space.

As illustrated on the facing page, if you open the **Custom Setup** properties for this effect, you'll find a 3D illustration of a sound space. As you adjust the knobs, the graphics will reshape to illustrate the changes you're making with regards to the distance from the object your sounds are bouncing off of, the absorption effect of other objects in the room, etc.

Although the **Reverb** effect is not available on the Mac version of Premiere Elements, a similar effect, **Delay**, can also be used to create an echo effect. To use **Delay** as an echo effect, open **Applied Effects** for your clip and set its properties and settings as follows:

Delay	Approximately 2-3 %
Feedback	Approximately 5
Mix	Approximately 25-30%

COOL TRICK

8 Make One Audio Channel into Stereo

If you use a microphone to record your audio – whether the microphone is plugged into your computer or into your camcorder's microphone jack – you often end up with the audio recorded to only one channel. Usually the left channel.

This is because most microphones record as monaural, or single channel of audio. Your camcorder, on the other hand, as well as your editing program works in stereo, or two channels of audio. This means, when you play back audio that's been recorded with a microphone, it often sounds weak, and you only hear it out of one speaker. Fortunately, Premiere Elements includes a feature for compensating for this.

1   Locate the Fill From Right effect

Click the **Effects** button on the **Toolbar**.

Under the **Audio** tab, click the **Category** bar at the top of the **Effects** panel (as illustrated on page 30) to drop-down the list of effects categories and, from it, select **Audio Effects**.

Make One Channel Audio Into Stereo

When your audio is recorded through a monaural microphone, it will be recorded only to the right audio channel, as indicated by blank left channel in your audio clip.

1. Locate Fill Right with Left in the Audio Effects.

2. Drag the effect onto a clip's audio.

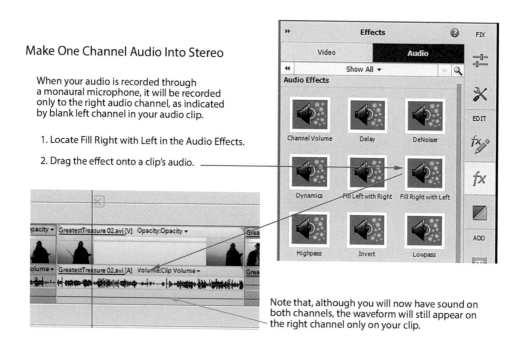

Note that, although you will now have sound on both channels, the waveform will still appear on the right channel only on your clip.

2   **Apply the Fill From Right effect**

Drag **Fill Right with Left** onto the clip on your timeline, as illustrated above.

The **Fill Right with Left** effect creates a virtual duplicate of the audio on the left stereo channel and uses it to fill the right channel. The result is that your audio will sound fuller and more like true stereo (even though, as illustrated above, the waveform on your clip will still only show sound on one channel).

COOL TRICK

9 Normalize Your Audio Level

Ideally, you'd like your audio to be more than just loud enough. You'd also like it to sound full, rich and clean.

And, although there is no substitute for having well recorded audio in the first place, Premiere Elements does include a professional-style tool for "**Normalizing**," or strengthening, your softer audio levels.

Normalizing raises the level of your audio. And, although it is also possible to raise your sound level by simply increasing its volume, **Normalizing** does this by raising the *audio gain* – in other words, increasing the level of the audio *source* rather than merely making it louder.

Normalize Your Audio Gain

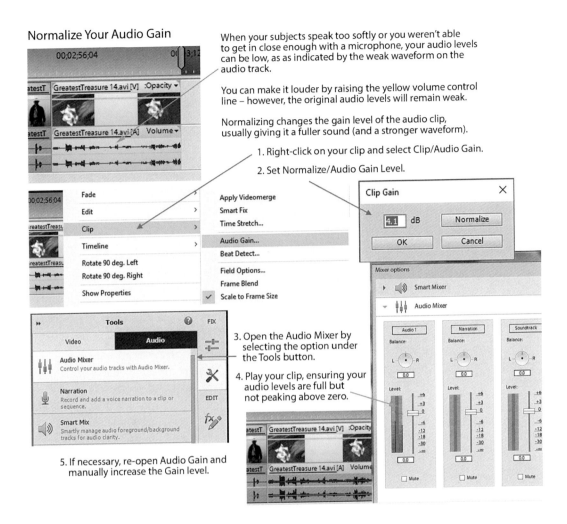

When your subjects speak too softly or you weren't able to get in close enough with a microphone, your audio levels can be low, as as indicated by the weak waveform on the audio track.

You can make it louder by raising the yellow volume control line – however, the original audio levels will remain weak.

Normalizing changes the gain level of the audio clip, usually giving it a fuller sound (and a stronger waveform).

1. Right-click on your clip and select Clip/Audio Gain.

2. Set Normalize/Audio Gain Level.

3. Open the Audio Mixer by selecting the option under the Tools button.

4. Play your clip, ensuring your audio levels are full but not peaking above zero.

5. If necessary, re-open Audio Gain and manually increase the Gain level.

It's a subtle difference – sort of like the difference between moving closer to your speakers and turning your stereo up louder. But, once you start using it, you may find yourself, like me, preferring to **Normalize** or raise your audio *gain* rather than merely raising the **Volume** level of your quieter audio clips.

1   **Open Audio Gain**

Right-click on the audio or audio/video clip you'd like to raise the audio levels for and, in the **Clip** sub-menu, select **Audio Gain**, as illustrated above.

2   **Set Normalize level**

The **Clip Gain** option panel will appear.

Click the **Normalize** button. The window will close and, ideally, the waveform indicating your clip's audio level will look fuller and stronger.

If it doesn't seem to have raised the audio level enough, re-open the **Clip Gain** panel and manually type in a higher decibel (db) level. For slightly weak audio, try a level of about 3. For very weak audio, try a level of 10 or more. Click **OK**.

Whenever you adjust the audio levels in your videos, it's best never to trust the sound coming out of your speakers. Premiere Elements' **Audio Mixer** is an excellent tool for precisely monitoring your project's audio levels.

3 Open the Audio Mixer

Click the **Tools** button on the **Toolbar** and, from the **Audio** category, select the **Audio Mixer**.

Although the **Audio Mixer** is primarily designed as a dynamic tool for adjusting your audio levels, its meters can also used to monitor the audio levels of your overall movie as well as its individual audio tracks.

4 Check your clip's audio levels

Drag the **CTI** (playhead) to the beginning of your clip and play your clip by either clicking the play button or by pressing the spacebar.

Watch your audio levels in the **Audio Mixer** and ensure that the sound registers between -6 and zero and *rarely or never peaks above zero*. Overly loud (or *"over-modulated"*) audio can sound distorted.

5 Tweak your Normalize/Audio Gain level

If necessary, **right-click** on your clip and again select **Audio Gain** and repeat the process until your clip's audio is strong but not over-modulated.

You can re-open and reset a clip's **Normalize/Audio Gain** level at any time while you're editing your project.

Eventually you'll get a feel for how much it takes to raise audio that's represented by certain audio waveform levels. I usually start with about 4 db to **Normalize** audio medium levels of audio and 10 db or more for audio that is very weak (say, a conversation recorded from several feet away).

Two things to remember about **Normalizing**, however. One is that, when you raise your audio gain, you raise the audio level for your *entire clip* – loud stuff as well as quite stuff. In other words, if you've got varying levels of sound going on in the same clip, you may need to slice it into manageable pieces (as described in the *Hot Tip* on page 33) or even use audio keyframes to control your sound levels at specific points in a clip.

The other thing to remember is that raising the **Audio Gain** for a clip raises the levels of *unwanted* audio as well as the audio you do want to make louder. In other words, although you can bring up the audio level of something spoken on the other side of a room, you'll be raising the audio levels of all of the other room noise also – so you still might not be able to hear what is being said.

Some audio simply can't be salvaged, unfortunately.

Chapter 4
Cool Tricks with Photos and Graphics
Adding life to still photos

Photos and other graphics can make great source files for your videos.

But just because your pictures are still photos doesn't mean they need to stand still!

With a little imagination (and a couple of cool tricks) you can add movement, and even depth, to your pictures and graphics.

There are many fun and exciting things you can do with your photos in Premiere Elements.

Sure, you can create a slideshow – but you can also add motion and even 3D movement to your photos and graphics to make them seem as living and real as any video.

A couple of these tricks will require a photo or graphic editing program to supplement Premiere Elements. I'll be walking you through creating these effects with Premiere Elements' sister program, **Photoshop Elements**. But these same effects can be accomplished using the professional version of Photoshop, Paint Shop Pro and quite likely even the excellent free, open source program Gimp.

COOL TRICK

10 Keyframe a Motion Path Pan & Zoom

The most basic (and yet always welcome) thing you can do to add interest to your photos and slideshows is to create motion paths over them. Motion paths are pans and zooms over your photos, often starting with a close-up of one detail and then slowly pulling back to reveal the rest of the photo (or vice versa).

There are, of course, generic pan and zoom **Preset Effects** which can be randomly placed on your photos to add some kind of movement – and this is better than nothing. Premiere Elements also includes a **Pan & Zoom Tool** for intuitively creating motion paths. But manually keyframing your motion paths gives you a lot more flexibility. Additionally, the process of keyframing is well worth getting to know, since it's a concept that shows up in many forms in Premiere Elements.

To add real excitement to your videos and slideshows, you'll want your movements to have meaning and to tell a story. To widen back, for instance, from a close-up of a man's smiling face to a wider shot of him standing next to his new car. Or to slowly zoom in from a photo of a bride and groom standing at the altar to a close-up of a tear in the groom's eye.

HOT TIP
Turn off the Scale to Frame Size preference!

Before you bring any photos or graphics into Premiere Elements, we recommend that you go to the program's **Edit** menu select **Preferences**. (On a Mac, select **Preferences** under the program name.) On the **General** page, *uncheck* the option to **Scale to Frame Size**.

When the **Scale to Frame Size** option is selected, the program will automatically scale any photos you add to the size of your video frame – a function that can get in the way of creating motion paths and having full control over your photo's scale or position.

Create a Motion Path (Part 1)

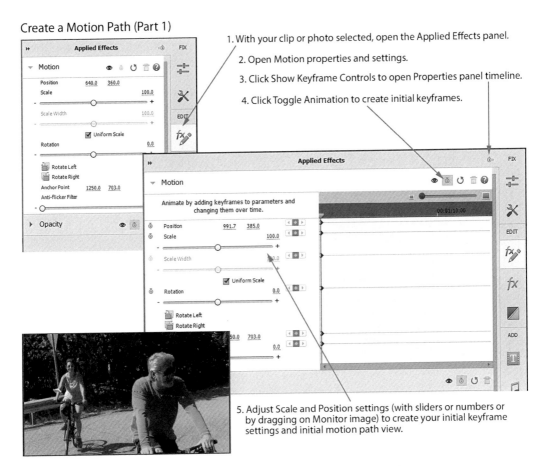

1. With your clip or photo selected, open the Applied Effects panel.

2. Open Motion properties and settings.

3. Click Show Keyframe Controls to open Properties panel timeline.

4. Click Toggle Animation to create initial keyframes.

5. Adjust Scale and Position settings (with sliders or numbers or by dragging on Monitor image) to create your initial keyframe settings and initial motion path view.

The basic principle of keyframing a motion path is pretty simple: You define two or more points (keyframes) which represent certain views of your photo, and Premiere Elements creates the animated motion path between them. In this *Cool Trick*, we'll create a basic two-keyframe move over our photo – although your actual motion paths can include any number of keyframes!

1 **Open the Applied Effects panel for your photo**

With a photo selected on your timeline, click the **Applied Effects** button on the right side of the program's interface.

The **Applied Effects** panel will open.

2 **Open the Motion properties**

Click the **Motion** listing to open its properties and settings.

Included among the properties are **Position**, which defines the center of your video frame, measured in pixels, and **Scale**, the percentage your clip is sized up or down (essentially, how much you're zoomed in or out on your photo or clip).

41

3 Show Keyframe Controls

Click the **Show Keyframe Controls** button (the stopwatch) in the upper right of the **Applied Effects** panel, as in the illustration on the previous page. A mini-timeline representing the duration of the clip on your timeline will appear to the right of the **Motion** properties and settings.

4 Toggle Animation to create initial keyframes

Move the **CTI** (playhead) on the **Applied Effects** panel timeline to the beginning of the clip. (The **CTI** on your main timeline will move in sync with it so that the results of any effects you add or settings you make will appear on your **Monitor** panel.)

Click **Toggle Animation** (the stopwatch icon to the right of the **Motion** properties listing, as illustrated on the previous page). A set of diamond-shaped keyframe points will be added to the **Applied Effects** panel timeline at the position of the **CTI**.

5 Create your initial keyframe settings

As long as your **CTI** remains directly over your keyframe points, the keyframe with automatically be updated with any changes you make to any settings.

Per the *Hot Tip* below, I've sized the photos in my example to 1000x750 pixels before I brought them into my standard definition video project. That means I have enough resolution to use **Scale** (zoom) settings from about 65% (a view of the complete photo) to just over 100% (zoom).

HOT TIP
Optimize your photo sizes for video

Despite the fact that it fills an entire TV screen, a standard definition video frame is really only the equivalent of a 640x480 pixel or an 855x480 pixel image. The process of a program, like Premiere Elements, taking your photos from whatever size you put in to video frame size is called downsampling. And, unfortunately, downsampling is something Premiere Elements does not do very efficiently. In fact, the larger the photo you put in, the more likely the program will slow to a crawl or even choke.

For this reason, we recommend that, before you bring any photos into a standard definition or DVD Premiere Elements projects, you use your graphics program to size the photos to no larger than 1000x750 pixels in size at 72 ppi. If you are working on a 1920x1080 high definition project, size your photos to 2500x1875 pixels.)

When your photos are this size, we've found, the program performs most efficiently. Your photos are large enough to allow room for some panning and zooming, and yet not large enough to challenge or choke the program's downsampling engine.

That said, also consider the advice in the *Hot Tip* on page 44.

Create a Motion Path (Part 2)

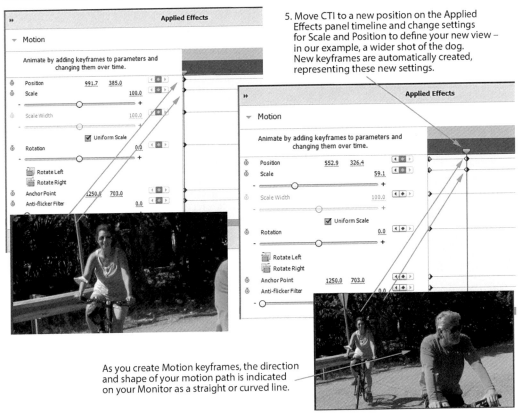

5. Move CTI to a new position on the Applied Effects panel timeline and change settings for Scale and Position to define your new view – in our example, a wider shot of the dog. New keyframes are automatically created, representing these new settings.

As you create Motion keyframes, the direction and shape of your motion path is indicated on your Monitor as a straight or curved line.

In my sample above, I want to keyframe a motion that begins in close-up and then pans out to show the entire photo, so I'll be using an initial **Scale** keyframe setting of 100%, which I set using the **Scale** slider.

Because I want to keep the dog in the center of the video frame, I need to adjust the **Position** just a bit. We could do this by changing the horizontal and vertical vectors for the center of the frame (the two numbers to the right of the **Position** listing which are, by default at 360 240, the center of a 720x480 video frame). However, I can also do this more intuitively by simply clicking on the image in the **Monitor** panel and dragging it into position. As I do, the **Position** numbers will register the change and it will automatically be applied to the existing keyframe.

By the way, you can also change the **Scale** of your image by dragging on the image in the **Monitor** panel. When you click on the image in the **Monitor**, corner handles will appear around the image and, by dragging the corners in or out, you can zoom into or back from your image.

The challenge in my particular situation is that, because my image is 1000x750 pixels in size and my video frame is 720x480 pixels in size, my corner handles are too far outside the frame for me to see without changing the **Monitor's** zoom level – which is why I've begun by setting my **Scale** numerically.

6   Create another set of keyframes

To create a second set of keyframes, move the **CTI** playhead to the end of the **Applied Effects** panel timeline and then change the **Scale** and **Position** settings. As you do, the program will automatically create new keyframes at the position of the **CTI** for this new **Scale** setting.

In my example, I adjusted my photo's **Scale** to 59%, zooming out from the close-up to show the entire photo. A new keyframe for **Scale** is created.

Because I changed the **Position** of the center of my photo in **Step 6**, my photo is now off-center in the video frame.

To reposition my image, I'll click on the image in the **Monitor** panel again and drag the photo to a position in which it fills the video frame. (I could also have typed in the centering **Position** numbers 360 240.) As I do, the program automatically creates a keyframe representing this new **Position** setting also.

And, voila! We've created a motion path!

The program will create the animation between the two keyframe points and, as the timeline plays, the **Monitor** will display a slow zoom back from a close up of the dog to a longer shot of him standing in the woods near the creek.

If this were a 1920x1080 pixel high-definition project and I was using a 2500x1875 pixel photo, my settings would be just a bit different.

My initial keyframe would have used a **Scale** of about 100% and an initial **Position** of about 1000 350. (See the *Hot Tip* below for a discussion of scaling a photo larger than 100%.)

HOT TIP
Optimized photo sizes are guidelines rather than rules

Although you can occasionally scale your photos larger than 100% when creating a pan and zoom effect, it's best to avoid doing so. Scaling a photo larger than its resolution can result in an "over-rezzed" or blurry slide.

So consider our 1000x750 or 2500x1875 recommended size for a photo a *guideline* rather than a rule. You can certainly use a slightly larger photo when necessary or, in a high definition video project, a photo as large as 3000x2250 pixels without overloading the program or negativing impacting the look of your slideshow.

Just know that the closer your photo is to your video's resolution, the more efficiently the program will be able to work with it and the sharper your final video slideshow will look.

My second keyframe would have a **Scale** of about 59% and the centering **Position** would have been 960 540.

Keyframe points can be added, edited, moved or removed. (The closer you move them together, the faster the animation between them.)

You can change and adjust their settings at any time. Keyframe points can even be copied (individually or as a group) and pasted into the properties for another clip or photo to duplicate the move or effect!

Keyframing is one of the most powerful tools in Premiere Elements, and learning the technique will take you a long way toward creating a number of special effects and animations. It's well worth getting to know, as it plays a role in a number of the *Cool Tricks* we cover in this book.

COOL TRICK

11 Use a Graphic to Frame Your Video

Graphics can be created in another program, such as Photoshop Elements, and brought into Premiere Elements for use in your videos. Most times you'll want those graphics or pictures to appear in your video as a rectangular, opaque image, such as a photo. But sometimes you'll want them to include transparent areas, so that this graphic can be placed on an upper video track and your video can show through it or be framed by it.

In this *Cool Trick*, we'll create a picture frame with a transparent center. The frame itself will become a border for our video frame, and our video will display through its open center.

1 **Create a new graphic file**

In Photoshop Elements, go to the **File** menu and select **New/Blank File**.

On the **New File** option screen that opens, select the **Film & Video Preset** then, from the **Size** drop-down menu, select either the **DV** or **DV Widescreen** option for a standard definition project or the **HDTV 1080p** option for a high-definition project, as illustrated on page 46.

Ensure that **Background Contents** is set to **Transparent**.

Click **OK**.

This will create a blank Photoshop Elements file with no layers and no background.

The light gray checkerboard pattern you see on this canvas indicates that the file is not only blank but also transparent.

Use a Graphic to Frame Your Video (Part 1)

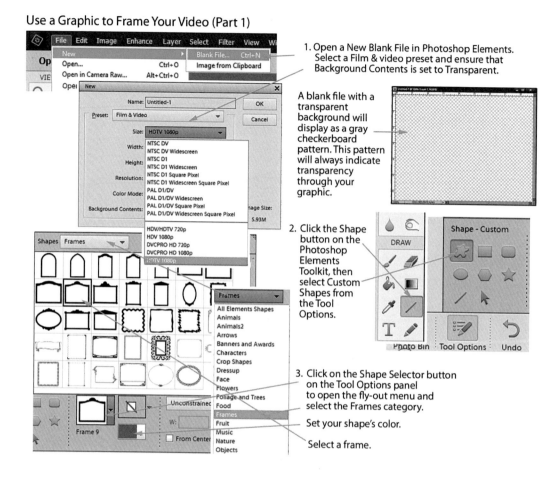

1. Open a New Blank File in Photoshop Elements. Select a Film & video preset and ensure that Background Contents is set to Transparent.

A blank file with a transparent background will display as a gray checkerboard pattern. This pattern will always indicate transparency through your graphic.

2. Click the Shape button on the Photoshop Elements Toolkit, then select Custom Shapes from the Tool Options.

3. Click on the Shape Selector button on the Tool Options panel to open the fly-out menu and select the Frames category.

Set your shape's color.

Select a frame.

2 Select the Custom Shape Tool

Click on the **Shape Tool** button on the Photoshop Elements Toolkit, along the left side of the editor workspace.

The shapes available for you to create with this tool will appear on the left side of the **Tool Options** panel, which appears below the program's Editor workspace.

Select the **Custom Shape Tool** from the **Tool Options** panel.

3 Select a frame shape

With the **Custom Shape Tool** selected, go to the **Tool Options** along the bottom of the Photoshop Elements interface.

As illustrated above, set the color for your frame in the shape options.

Then click on the **Shape Selector** button to open the **Custom Shapes** fly-out menu. Click the drop-down menu at the top of this fly-out menu and select the **Frames** category.

Click to select a frame.

Use a Graphic to Frame Your Video (Part 2)

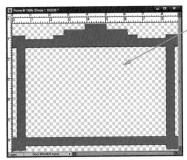

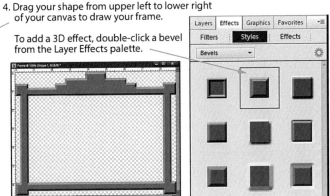

4. Drag your shape from upper left to lower right of your canvas to draw your frame.

To add a 3D effect, double-click a bevel from the Layer Effects palette.

5. Save your frame as a PSD.

6. Use Add Media/Files and Folders to import your frame graphic into a Premiere Elements project.

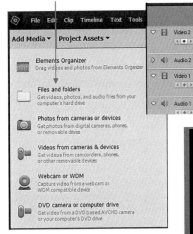

7. Place the video clip you want to frame on the Video 1 track of your timeline.

8. Place your frame graphic on Video 2, above the clip you want to frame. Extend it as necessary to match your video's duration.

9. Adjust Position and Scale in the Motion properties on the Applied Effects panel so that your video fits inside the frame.

4 Create your frame graphic

Click and drag from the upper left corner to lower right corner of your blank graphic file to draw your frame shape. You can click on the frame shape again and drag on its corner handles to resize and reshape it.

To make our frame look 3D, go to the **Effects** panel in the Photoshop Elements **Panel Bin** (to the right of the Editor space) and click on the **Styles** button, as illustrated above. (If the **Effects** panel isn't visible, select the option from the program's **Window** menu.) Select **Bevels** from the **Effects/Styles** panel's drop-down menu.

Double-click on one of the bevels to apply a 3D beveling effect to your frame.

5 **Save your frame as a PSD**

Go to the Photoshop Elements **File** menu and select **Save**. Save your file as a Photoshop PSD file. (PSDs are one of the few file formats that maintain transparency around your graphic.)

6 **Import the PSD into your video project**

In Premiere Elements, click the **Add Media** button in the upper left of the program and select the **Files and Folders** option.

Browse to locate the frame PSD you created above, select it and click **OK**.

The PSD will be added to your video project.

7 **Place the video to be framed on Video 1**

If your video is not already on your timeline, drag it from the **Project Assets** panel to the Video 1 track.

8 **Place your frame graphic on Video 2**

Drag the frame graphic we created in Photoshop Elements from **Project Assets** to the Video 2 track, directly above your main video. Click and drag the ends of the frame graphic clip on the timeline to extend it so that it covers the duration of your entire video clip.

Your frame should appear over your video in the **Monitor**.

HOT TIP
Square vs. non-square pixels

Unlike photos, standard definition video uses non-square pixels (the tiny little blocks of color) to create your image. In NTSC, these video pixels are only 90% as wide as they are tall. This is how a 720x480 video frame creates a 4:3 image. In widescreen, the pixels are 120% as wide as they are tall – so those same 720x480 pixels make a 16:9 image!

Your photos and graphics will most likely use square pixels which, when added to your video project, will automatically become non-square video pixels.

Here are the square pixel measurements you should use for creating full-screen graphics and photos for your video projects:

Standard 4:3 NTSC video	640x480 pixels
Widescreen 16:9 NTSC video	855x480 pixels
Standard 4:3 PAL video	768x576 pixels
Widescreen 16:9 PAL video	1024x576 pixels

Modern high-definition video, on the other hand, uses square pixels to creates its images. So, to create full-screen graphics for a high-definition video, use this picture size:

High-definition video	1920x1080 pixels
UHD 4K video	3840x2160 pixels

9 **Scale your video to fit inside the frame**

To scale your video so that it appears inside the frame, click to select the video clip to be framed on your timeline and then click the **Applied Effects** button.

In the **Applied Effects** panel, click on the **Motion** listing to open the **Motion** properties and settings.

Use the slider to adjust the **Scale**. Then tweak the **Position** settings so that your video fits neatly inside your frame.

Rather than creating your own frame in Photoshop Elements, you can also use clip art of a frame or even a photo or scan of an *actual* picture frame to frame your video.

The key to creating a graphic that includes transparent areas is ensuring that the graphic you are using is on a *floating layer* rather than a *background layer* in Photoshop Elements. (Most graphics and photos, when opened in Photoshop Elements, do not include layers and will appear as a background layer only.)

To convert a background layer to a floating layer, **double-click** on the background layer on the **Layers** panel in Photoshop Elements. This will trigger Photoshop Elements to change the name of the layer from **Background** to **Layer 0.**

Once your background has become a floating layer, any areas you select and delete from the photo will become transparent.

If you then save this file as a PSD, these deleted areas will remain transparent when the file is imported into a Premiere Elements video project.

COOL TRICK

12 Add Motion Behind Your Slideshow

You can achieve some interesting effects combining more than one video source in your frame. **Motion backgrounds** – colorful, moving, usually looping 3D imagery – create an interesting effect when combined with another video source. Adding a motion background behind your photos can add a whole new dimension to a simple slideshow (as you can see in the illustration on the following page).

Muvipix.com offers dozens of motion backgrounds, by the way – many of them absolutely free. Chances are we'll have one in the very style and theme you're looking for!

Add Motion Behind Your Slideshow

1. Place your motion background on Video 1.

2. Place your photo(s) on Video 2, above your motion background.

3. With a photo selected, open the Applied Effects panel by clicking the button on the right side of the interface.

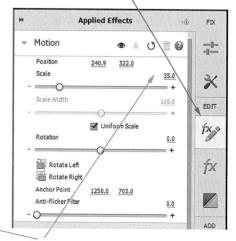

4. Scale and position your photo so that it floats over the motion background.

To make for an interesting composition, drag your photos to various positions over the background and add fades in and out for each.

1 Place your motion background on Video 1

Drag your motion background to the Video 1 track.

Most motion background clips are brief, but their motion tends to be somewhat repetitive – so you can add as many copies of a motion background clip as you need to your timeline, one following the other, to create a seamlessly looping background.

2 Place your photo on Video 2

Drag your photo to the Video 2 track, above your motion background. Your photo will likely fill the screen and hide the video on Video 1.

3 Open your photo's Applied Effects panel

Click to select the photo on your timeline and select **Applied Effects** button on the right side of the interface.

The **Applied Effects** panel for this clip will open.

4 Scale your photo

Click on the **Motion** listing to open the **Motion** properties.

> Use the **Scale** slider to reduce the size of the photo. If you've
> optimized your photo, per our recommendations, to 1000x750
> pixels in size (or 2500x1875 for high-def), a **Scale** of about 30-40%
> should give you a nice mix of photo and motion background.

To make the composition of your frame more interesting, click on the photo in
your **Monitor** panel and drag it off from the center of the frame, as I did in my
illustration.

By right-clicking on your photo clip on your timeline, you can select the options
for adding a **Fade In** and **Fade Out** to the picture.

Continue to add your photos (with fades in and out), placing them at a variety
of positions around the video frame, to create a dynamic and exciting slideshow
over your looping motion background.

COOL TRICK

13 Make Your Photo Look 3D

This is one of the coolest effects you'll find in this book (and also one of the
most elaborate). In fact, you'll see a lot or pros using this very cool trick. I've
noticed a lot of TV networks using it in promos for their shows.

I learned this "parallax effect" trick from Paul LS on the **Muvipix** forums. The
effect is as if your photo has become 3-dimensional, with the elements in the
picture moving separately as we pan and zoom into it.

How many levels you add to this effect is up to you. But even just splitting your
photo into two levels makes for a very cool effect!

The trick is in how you prepare your photo – and it is pretty Photoshop
Elements-intensive. If you're unfamiliar with selecting and cloning in Photoshop
Elements, you may want to check out some of the tutorials online or see my
book, *The Muvipix.com Guide to Photoshop Elements 2018,* available on the
Muvipix site and from Amazon.com.

1 **Select your photo's foreground elements**

   Before you begin, ensure that your original photo is 1000x750 pixels
   in size. (2500x1875 for high-definition video.)

   With your photo open in the Photoshop Elements editor workspace,
   draw a selection around your foreground elements.

I have chosen for my photo a picture of an Italian village on a hillside. I will be
using the village and the hillside as my foreground layer and the mountains
behind the village as my background layer.

Make Your Photo Look 3D (part 1)

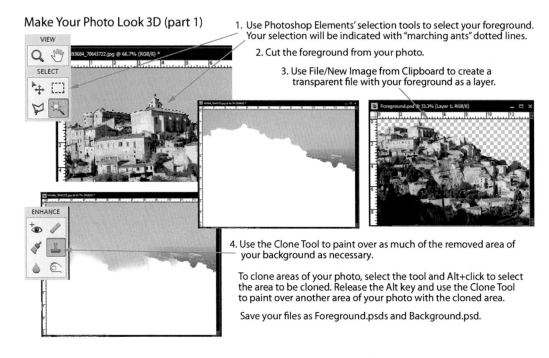

1. Use Photoshop Elements' selection tools to select your foreground. Your selection will be indicated with "marching ants" dotted lines.

2. Cut the foreground from your photo.

3. Use File/New Image from Clipboard to create a transparent file with your foreground as a layer.

4. Use the Clone Tool to paint over as much of the removed area of your background as necessary.

To clone areas of your photo, select the tool and Alt+click to select the area to be cloned. Release the Alt key and use the Clone Tool to paint over another area of your photo with the cloned area.

Save your files as Foreground.psds and Background.psd.

There are a number of selection tools in Photoshop Elements – from the **Magic Wand**, which selects everything within a range of colors, to brushes, which select what you "paint" over.

The process of "selecting" draws a moving dotted line (known in the industry as "marching ants") around various objects or areas in your photo. When an area is selected, it is isolated, and you can apply effects to it or cut it from the rest of the photo.

If you're not a skilled Photoshop Elements user, you can stick with the basics. The **Polygonal Lasso Tool** draws a selected connect-the-dots style selection as you click to create a path.

Once you've drawn a selection, you can add to it by holding down the **Shift** key as you click to draw an additional selection.

If you'd like to unselect and area you've previously selected, you can remove from it by holding down the **Alt** key as you use a selection tool to draw a de-selection.

2   **Cut your selected area**

With your photo open in the Photoshop Elements editor, cut your selection by going to the **Edit** menu and selecting **Cut** or by pressing **Ctrl+x** (⌘+x on a Mac).

3   **Create new image from clip**

Go to the **New** menu and select **Image from Clipboard**.

A new Photoshop Elements file will be created and the image on your clipboard (the selection cut from your photo) will automatically be pasted into it.

The gray checkerboard pattern behind your image is an indication that your image's background is transparent.

If you'd like, at this point you can select the **Eraser Tool** from the Photoshop Elements Toolkit and clean up the edges of your image.

Save your file as a Photoshop PSD file. Name it "Foreground." (You must save this file as a PSD in order for it to maintain its transparent background.)

Close the file.

4   Fill in the background on your original file

Go back to your original photo – which now has a white silhouette where your foreground used to be.

Select the **Clone Tool** on the Photoshop Elements Toolkit.

The **Clone Tool** will copy elements from one area of your photo and use them to paint over another area of your photo.

Hold down the **Alt/Option** key and click on the area of your photo you'd like to clone. We're going to try to paint in the area we just cut from this photo so that it appears to be part of the existing background.

Once you've selected the area to be cloned, release the **Alt** key and click and drag to paint in the silhouette.

You may not need to paint in the entire white area. But, as in my illustration on the previous page, you will need to ensure that you paint/clone over enough of it so that the parts you've removed don't show when you create your motion path animation in Premiere Elements.

This may take some work, and you may have to **Alt-click** to redefine a cloned area and repaint/clone a number of times to fill it all in and make it look natural. Naturally, plain and undefined backgrounds, like skies, trees and oceans, are the easiest to clone.

As an alternative to cloning the background, you can always, of course, use a completely separate photo as your background.

When you're done, save this file as a PSD. Name it "Background."

By saving your files as PSD files, you have saved them with their transparent areas intact. When you import PSD files into Premiere Elements, Premiere Elements will display their transparent areas as transparent.

Make Your Photo Look 3D (Part 2)

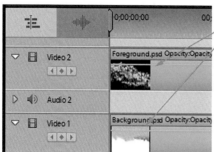

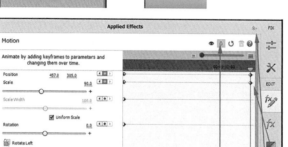

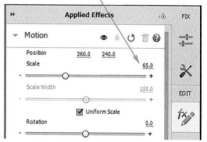

5. Use Add Media/Files and Folders to import your photos.

6. Place Background.psd on Video 1 and Foreground.psd on Video 2, directly above it.

7. With Background.psd selected on your timeline, open the Applied Effects panel by clicking the button on the right side of the interface.

Click to open the Motion properties and set the Scale to 65%.

8. With the Applied Effects panel still open, select Foreground.psd on your timeline.

Click to open the Motion properties and set the Scale to 65%.

9. Click the Show Keyframes Controls button (stopwatch).

Move the CTI to the beginning of the clip and click Toggle Animation to create an initial keyframe.

10. Move the CTI to the end of the clip and set Scale to 90%. Click on the Monitor and drag the Foreground image slightly down and to one side. New keyframes will automatically be created for Scale and Position.

Because the Foreground and Background change scale and position separately, they appear to be moving on separate 3D planes!

5 Import your PSD files into Premiere Elements

Go to Premiere Elements' **Preferences** (under the **Edit** menu on a PC). On the **General** page, ensure that S**cale to Frame Size** is *unchecked*. Click **OK**.

Click on **Add Media** and select **PC Files and Folders**. Browse to locate "Foreground.psd" and "Background.psd" and add them to your project.

6 Layer the photos on your timeline

Place Background.psd on your timeline on the Video 1 track.

Place Foreground.psd on your timeline on the Video 2 track, directly above Background.psd on the timeline, as illustrated above.

The two images should combine in the **Monitor** panel to look something very similar to your original photograph – although, if you've sized your original photo to 1000x750 pixels (or 2500x1875 for high-def), as we've recommended, the images will likely be so large that you'll only see a portion of this composition in the **Monitor**.

7 **Scale your background image**

Click to select Background.psd on your timeline and open the **Applied Effects** panel by clicking the button on the right of the interface..

Click on the **Motion** listing in the **Applied Effects** panel to open the **Motion** properties and settings.

Set the **Scale** for Background.psd to 65% for a standard definition project or about 95% for a high-def project so that it fills the video frame.

8 **Scale your foreground image**

Select the Foreground.psd on your timeline and again click on the **Motion** listing in the **Applied Effects** panel to open the **Motion** properties and settings.

Set the **Scale** for Foreground.psd to 65% for a standard definition project or about 95% for a high-def project.

If you'd like to adjust the position of Foreground.psd, click on it in the **Monitor** panel and drag it into place.

The image in your **Monitor** – revealing the two photos layered one over the other – should now be very close to your original photo's composition.

9 **Create an initial keyframe for Foreground.psd**

As detailed in *Cool Trick 14,* click on the **Show Keyframe Controls** button (the stopwatch) in the upper right of the panel to open the **Applied Effects** panel's mini-timeline.

Position the **CTI** (playhead) at the beginning of the clip.

Click the **Toggle Animation** (stopwatch) button to the right of the **Motion** listing to create your initial **Motion** keyframes.

10 **Create a motion path keyframe**

Move the **CTI** on the **Applied Effect** panel's timeline to the end of the clip.

Set **Scale** to 90% for a standard definition project to 110% for a high-def. A new keyframe point will automatically be created at the position of the **CTI**.

Click on your foreground image in the **Monitor** and drag it slightly to the side and down. A **Position** keyframe will be automatically created at the position of the **CTI**.

When you play back your clip, the Foreground image will appear to move toward the camera and to the side, as if you are moving through 3D space toward and around it. The Background image will remain in place (although you can add some motion to it, too, if you'd like).

The result should be as if you are moving into the photo, with its elements changing position in three-dimensional space.

There are a number of ways to take this effect even further, if you're ambitious enough. You can add or even keyframe a **Blur** effect to the Background clip to give the illusion of depth of field.

And, if you're really ambitious, you can cut out several layers of elements from your photo – each appearing on a separate video track, each using a slightly different level of keyframed motion – to really create a *deep* 3D illusion! (We use three layers in the demo tutorial on the Muvipix.com web page.)

Chapter 5
Cool Keyframing Tricks
Effects that move and change

When you add keyframing to your effects, you change them from static, simple effects to moving, animated special effects that change shape, position and intensity over time.

With keyframing you can turn your out-of-the-box effects into something way outside the box!

Keyframing is the process of creating special effects in Premiere Elements by defining the settings for an effect or property at two or more points in time in order to create an animation or transition between them.

As we demonstrate in **Chapter 4, Cool Tricks with Photos and Graphics**, keyframing can add motion, and even dimension, to a still photo. It can also be used to create effects that vary their intensity over the course of a clip.

With keyframing, for instance, you can dissolve from a video with no effects applied to it into an old movie effect.

With keyframing, you can send your video tumbling through 3D space.

With keyframing, you can create settings for the **Crop** effect so that the cropping becomes animated, opening or closing to reveal different areas of your video.

COOL TRICK

14 Dissolve from a Modern to an Old Film Effect

Keyframing can not only be used to create an animation between positions for your clips and effects, but it can also be used to vary the intensity of an effect. You can, for instance, use keyframing to make your video go from clear to blurred or from normal to an intense twirl.

In this *Cool Trick*, we'll take the **Old Film** effect and keyframe it so that our video dissolves from a normal, modern clip into something that looks like an ancient, faded old movie.

1   **Locate the Old film effect**

Click the **Effects** button on the **Toolbar.**

The **Old Film** effect is located in the **NewBlue FilmLook** category of **Video Effects**.

2   **Apply the Old Film effect**

Drag the **Old Film** effect from the **Effects** panel onto a clip on your timeline.

If the **CTI** (playhead) is over this clip on your timeline, your video should immediately look like an old, tattered and yellowed movie.

3   **Open the clip's Applied Effects panel**

With the clip selected on your timeline, click the **Applied Effects** button on the right side of the interface.

Dissolve from Modern to an Old Film Effect

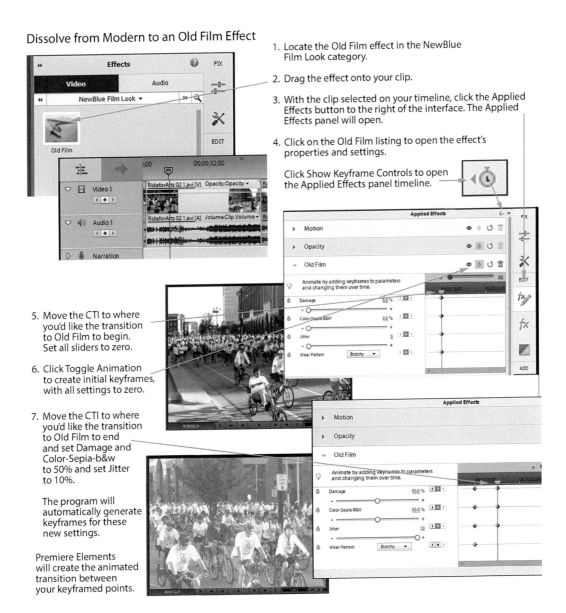

1. Locate the Old Film effect in the NewBlue Film Look category.

2. Drag the effect onto your clip.

3. With the clip selected on your timeline, click the Applied Effects button to the right of the interface. The Applied Effects panel will open.

4. Click on the Old Film listing to open the effect's properties and settings.

   Click Show Keyframe Controls to open the Applied Effects panel timeline.

5. Move the CTI to where you'd like the transition to Old Film to begin. Set all sliders to zero.

6. Click Toggle Animation to create initial keyframes, with all settings to zero.

7. Move the CTI to where you'd like the transition to Old Film to end and set Damage and Color-Sepia-b&w to 50% and set Jitter to 10%.

   The program will automatically generate keyframes for these new settings.

   Premiere Elements will create the animated transition between your keyframed points.

4   Adjust the Old Film effect for your clip

Click on the **Old Film** effect listing on the **Applied Effects** panel to open the effect's properties and settings.

By default, the **Applied Effects** panel's keyframing workspace is hidden. To open it, click the **Show Keyframe Controls** button (the stopwatch) in the upper right of the panel, as in the illustration above.

5   Create your initial keyframe settings

Move the sliders for **Damage, Color-Sepia-b&w** and **Jitter** to zero.

In the **Monitor** panel, it should appear that your **Old Film** effect has been completely removed from your clip.

This will be our initial keyframe setting, which means that, up until this point in our clip, the video will appear to have no **Old Film** effect applied to it.

6   Toggle Animation to create initial keyframes

Move the **CTI** (playhead) on the **Applied Effects** panel timeline to the point in your clip at which you'd like your dissolve to **Old Film** to begin. (The **CTI** on your main timeline will move in sync with it so that the results of any effects you add or settings you change will appear on the **Monitor.**)

Click **Toggle Animation**, the stopwatch icon to the right of the **Old Film** effect listing. A set of diamond-shaped keyframe points representing each of this effect's properties and settings will be added to the **Applied Effects** panel timeline at the position of the **CTI,** as in the illustration on the previous page.

7   Create another set of keyframes

Now move the **CTI** down the **Applied Effects** panel timeline a few seconds (depending on how long you'd like your transition to the **Old Film** look to take).

Adjust the **Damage, Color-Sepia-b&w** and **Jitter** sliders so that the **Old Film** effect levels you'd like your video to have appear in the **Monitor** panel.

(Setting **Damage** and **Color-Sepia-b&w** to 50% and **Jitter** to 10% should produce a good effect.)

The program will automatically add keyframe points at the position of the **CTI.**

When you play your clip, your video will begin with a clean, modern look and then, beginning at the point of your first set of keyframes, it will dissolve into a very old, ragged movie.

(Because this is a relatively intense effect, you may want to render your timeline first, by pressing **Enter,** so that you can see it displayed at full quality.)

As with any keyframed effect, if you drag the keyframes closer together the transition will happen more quickly and if you drag them further apart the transition will happen more slowly.

And, naturally, you can rearrange your keyframes so that, rather than dissolving from modern look to old film, it dissolves from old film to modern.

COOL TRICK

15 Make Your Video Tumble Through Space

By combining one of Premiere Elements' 3D effects and a little keyframing magic, you can make your video appear to tumble toward or away from your viewer. It's definitely an attention-getting way of transitioning into movie!

In my demo, I'll be taking you through the steps of tumbling the video *into* your video frame. But, of course, if you reverse the keyframes and place them at the end of your clip, you can use the same steps to make your video tumble *away*.

1   **Locate the Basic 3D effect**

Click the **Effects** button on the **Toolbar**.

The **Basic 3D** effect is located in the **Perspective** category of **Video Effects**.

2   **Apply the Basic 3D effect**

Drag the effect from the **Effects** panel onto a clip on your timeline.

In the **Monitor**, your video should appear slightly skewed by the effect.

3   **Open the clip's Applied Effects panel**

With the clip selected on your timeline, click the **Applied Effects** button on the right side of the interface.

4   **Adjust the Basic 3D effect for your clip**

Click on the **Basic 3D** effect listing on the **Applied Effects** panel to open the effect's properties and settings.

By default, the **Applied Effects** panel's keyframing workspace is hidden. To open it, click the **Show Keyframe Controls** button (the stopwatch) in the upper right of the panel, as in the illustration on the following page.

5   **Toggle Animation to create initial keyframes**

Move the **CTI** (playhead) on the **Applied Effects** panel timeline to the very beginning of your clip. (The **CTI** on your main timeline will move in sync with it so that the results of any effects you add or settings you make will appear in your **Monitor**.)

Make Your Video Tumble Through Space

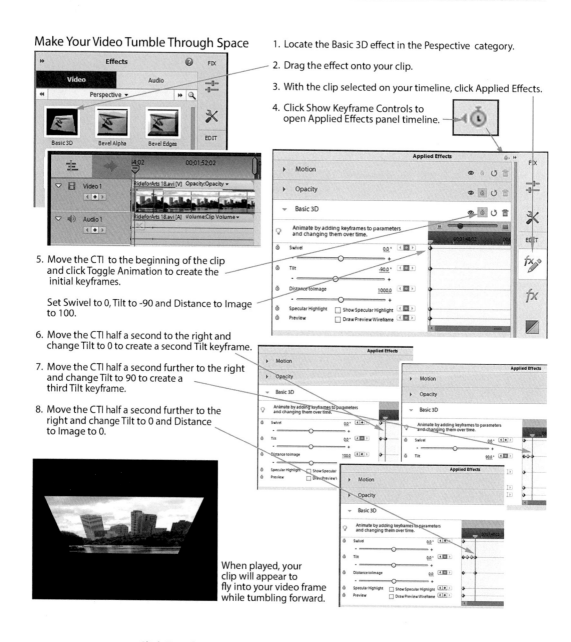

1. Locate the Basic 3D effect in the Pespective category.

2. Drag the effect onto your clip.

3. With the clip selected on your timeline, click Applied Effects.

4. Click Show Keyframe Controls to open Applied Effects panel timeline.

5. Move the CTI to the beginning of the clip and click Toggle Animation to create the initial keyframes.

    Set Swivel to 0, Tilt to -90 and Distance to Image to 100.

6. Move the CTI half a second to the right and change Tilt to 0 to create a second Tilt keyframe.

7. Move the CTI half a second further to the right and change Tilt to 90 to create a third Tilt keyframe.

8. Move the CTI half a second further to the right and change Tilt to 0 and Distance to Image to 0.

When played, your clip will appear to fly into your video frame while tumbling forward.

Click **Toggle Animation**, the stopwatch icon to the right of the **Basic 3D** effect listing. A set of diamond-shaped keyframe points representing each of the effect's properties settings will be added to the **Applied Effects** panel timeline at the position of the **CTI**.

6   Create your initial keyframe settings

As long as your **CTI** remains directly over your keyframe points, any adjustments you make to the effect's settings will be updated in the keyframe(s).

Set **Swivel** to 0 degrees.

Set **Tilt** to -90 degrees. This will make your video appear to be lying flat on its back.

Set **Distance to Image** to 1000. Your clip should now be virtually invisible.

7   Create a second Tilt keyframe

Now move the **CTI** down the **Applied Effects** panel timeline about half a second, as in the illustration.

Change **Tilt** to 0 degrees. Your clip will appear very small in the **Monitor** and a keyframe point will automatically be created at the position of the **CTI** on the **Applied Effects** panel timeline.

8   Create a third Tilt keyframe

Move the **CTI** another half second down the **Applied Effects** panel timeline.

Change **Tilt** to 90 degrees. Your clip will likely disappear again (it will actually be tilted forward), and a new keyframe point will be automatically created at the position of the **CTI**.

9   Create a final set of keyframes

Finally, move the **CTI** another half second down the **Applied Effects** panel timeline.

Change **Tilt** to 0 degrees.
Change **Distance to Image** to 0.

New keyframe points will be created for **Tilt** and **Distance to Image**, and your clip should now fill your video frame.

When you play your clip, your video will seem to be flying in from a long way off, tumbling forward through space before filling your video frame. (If your video isn't clear, you can render it, by pressing **Enter**, so that the program can display a high-quality version.)

You can speed up or slow down the animation by moving the keyframe points closer together or further apart from each other. And, of course, by creating additional **Tilt** keyframes, you can make the video tumble head over heels several times as it flies into the video frame!

HOT TIP
Keyframes are easily adjustable

The most powerful characteristic of keyframes is how easily adjustable they are.

The little diamonds that represent your keyframed positioned can be added at any point in your project, moved around, copied and deleted. The closer they are to each other, the faster the animation between them.

You can even vary the shape and speed of the animations between them by right-clicking on these little diamonds and selecting an interpolation method, such as **Ease In** or **Ease Out**.

16 Create an Animated Crop Wipe

Just as you can use keyframing to vary the intensity of an effect's properties, you can also use it to vary the shape, size or motion of an effect over the duration of a clip.

In this *Cool Trick*, we're going to take the **Crop** effect and apply keyframing to it so that the shape of the cropped area changes over time, essentially revealing different areas of our video frame over the duration of the clip.

1   **Locate the Crop effect**

Click the **Effects** button on the **Toolbar**.

The **Crop** effect is located in the **Transform** category of **Video Effects**.

2   **Apply the Crop effect**

Drag the effect from the **Effects** panel onto a clip on your timeline.

In the **Monitor**, your clip will appear cropped to the effect's default settings – **Left** 0%, **Top** 9%, **Right** 14% and **Bottom** 20%

3   **Open the clip's Applied Effects panel**

With the clip selected on the timeline, click the **Applied Effects** button on the right side of the interface.

Click on the **Crop** effect listing on the **Applied Effects** panel to open its properties and settings.

4   **Open the Applied Effects panel timeline**

By default, the **Applied Effects** panel's keyframing workspace is hidden. To open it, click the **Show Keyframe Controls** button (the stopwatch) in the upper right of the panel, as in the illustration on the facing page.

5   **Create an initial Crop position**

In my example, my goal is to begin with the clip cropped down to isolate a view of the woman on the beach. I will then keyframe the **Crop** effect to widen the shot to include the dog, then further widen it to reveal the entire shot of the beach.

To create this animation, I will need three sets of keyframes.

As with most effects, you can adjust the settings for the **Crop** effect either by using the sliders and/or number settings in the **Applied Effects** panel or, more intuitively, right on the **Monitor** panel, as illustrated.

Create a Crop Wipe

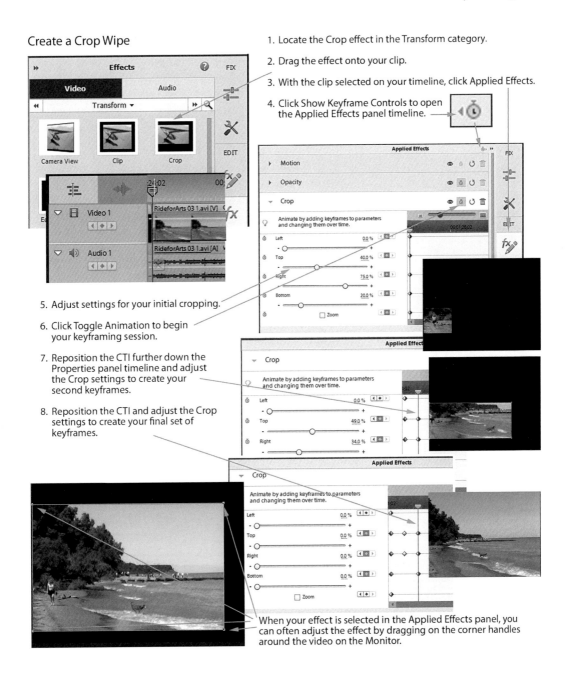

1. Locate the Crop effect in the Transform category.

2. Drag the effect onto your clip.

3. With the clip selected on your timeline, click Applied Effects.

4. Click Show Keyframe Controls to open the Applied Effects panel timeline.

5. Adjust settings for your initial cropping.

6. Click Toggle Animation to begin your keyframing session.

7. Reposition the CTI further down the Properties panel timeline and adjust the Crop settings to create your second keyframes.

8. Reposition the CTI and adjust the Crop settings to create your final set of keyframes.

When your effect is selected in the Applied Effects panel, you can often adjust the effect by dragging on the corner handles around the video on the Monitor.

To adjust the effect on the **Monitor** panel, click to select the **Crop** effect listing in the **Applied Effects** panel. Corner handles will then appear around the cropped area in the **Monitor**. By dragging on these corner handles, you can adjust the size and shape of the cropping.

The sliders and numbers in the **Applied Effects** panel will reflect these adjustments.

6   **Toggle Animation to create initial keyframes**

Move the **CTI** (playhead) on the **Applied Effects** panel timeline to the very beginning of your clip. (The **CTI** on your main timeline will move in sync with it so that the results of any effects you add or settings you make will appear on your **Monitor** panel.)

Click **Toggle Animation**, the stopwatch icon to the right of the **Crop** properties listing. A set of keyframe points representing each of this effect's properties will be added to the **Applied Effects** panel timeline at the position of the **CTI**. These keyframe points represent the initial setting for your **Crop** effect.

7   **Create a second set of Crop keyframes**

Now move the **CTI** down the **Applied Effects** panel timeline a second or so to the right (or however long you'd like your animation to last).

Again click on the **Crop** listing in the **Applied Effects** panel and drag the corner handles that appear around your video in the **Monitor** (or manually adjust the sliders) to create your second keyframed setting.

In my case, I've widened the cropping so that the dog is now included in the video frame.

Whenever you reposition the **CTI** and then change an effect's settings, new keyframe points will be automatically created on the **Applied** panel timeline.

HOT TIP
Cropping, Clipping and Zooming

At first glance, the **Crop** and **Clip** effects seems to do essentially the same thing – trim off the sides of your video clip. However, *how* they trim the sides is quite different.

When you **Clip** off the sides of a clip, you replace that side with a fill color, which you can designate in the effect's properties.

But, when you **Crop** off the sides of a clip, you leave transparency, revealing whatever happens to be on the video track or tracks below it on the timeline.

The **Crop** effect also includes an option in its properties to **Zoom**. Checking this **Zoom** option will expand the cropped area in your video so that it fills your video frame.

8   Create a final set of Crop keyframes

Now move the **CTI further** down the **Applied Effects** panel timeline, to the position you'd like your animation to end.

As we did in **Step 7**, make a final adjustment to your **Crop** effect, either by using the sliders and numbers or by clicking on the effect's listing in the **Applied Effects** panel and dragging on the corner handles which appear around your video on your **Monitor** panel.

In my case, I set all of my sliders to zero for this final keyframe, revealing my entire video in my video frame.

New keyframes are automatically added at the position of the **CTI** on the **Applied** panel timeline.

When you play your clip, your **Crop** effect will appear animated. In my case, this animation begins with my video frame black except for the cropped image of the woman in the lower left corner, then widening to show the dog, then finally un-cropping completely to show the entire video frame.

There are a number of interesting ways to use a keyframed **Crop** effect.

If you stack several clips, one above the other on your timeline on separate video tracks – each with its own keyframed **Crop** effect – you can create sort of a 1960s-style video collage of split screens in your video frame. (Think the *Woodstock* movie or the original *Thomas Crown Affair*).

You can also place your animated crop video in the Video 2 track, with a color matte or other motion background on Video 1 below it, so that your animated cropping appears over an interesting background rather than just black.

And, of course, using an animated, keyframed **Crop** effect, you can create your own custom transition, cropping your way out of one scene and into another.

Chapter 6
Cool Transition Tricks
Interesting ways to get from one clip to another

Sometimes you want to transition from one clip to another almost invisibly. It's then that a simple cut or subtle dissolve is in order.

But other times you want to have a little fun – to create your own, custom transitions. And with Premiere Elements, there are a number of very cool ways to do this.

Premiere Elements comes loaded with over 100 transitions, from basic dissolves to pushes, curtains, bars and stripes. And they alone can take you a long way. But for the very cool, there are ways to go beyond the standard, pre-packaged transitions, and create some interesting and custom ways to get from clip to clip.

COOL TRICK

17 Use a Preset as a Transition

Usually, when you want to add a transition between two clips, you go to the **Transitions** panel and grab one from the over 100 audio or video transitions included in the program.

But, although the program provides a great library of transitions to choose from, you're by no means limited to this set. A number of **Presets** are designed to be used as transitions also. (And, you can even create your own!)

1   Locate the Twirl Out preset effect

Click the **Effects** button on the **Toolbar**.

The **Twirl Out** effect is located in the **Presets** category of **Video Effects**, in the **Twirls** sub-category.

2   Apply the Twirl Out effect to Clip 1

Drag the **Twirl Out** preset effect onto the clip you would like to transition from (Clip 1).

Twirl Out automatically attaches to the *end* of a clip. Its pre-keyframed settings transition the last second of the clip from no effect to a 4x twirl.

3   Apply the Twirl In effect to Clip 2

Drag the **Twirl In** preset effect onto the clip you would like to transition to (Clip 2).

Twirl In automatically attaches to the *beginning* of a clip. Its pre-keyframed settings transition the first second of a clip from a 4x twirl to no effect.

And that's really all there is to it! When you play your video, Clip 1 will end by spinning into a full twirl – and, when you spin out of the twirl, you'll be in Clip 2!

There are a couple of **Presets** that work well as transitions, each identified by the words "in" and "out" in their names. They are **Fast Blur In/Fast Blur Out, Mosaic In/Mosaic Out, Solarize In/Solarize Out** and, as we've seen, **Twirl In/Twirl Out**. In addition, a number of the **PiP** (Picture-in-Picture) **Presets** include animations that slide, zoom or spin your **PiP** video in or out of the video frame – essentially transitioning the inset video into or out of your movie.

Use a Preset as a Transition

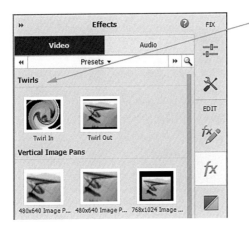

1. Locate the Twirls in the Preset Effects.

2. Apply Twirl Out to outgoing Clip 1.

3. Apply Twirl In to incoming Clip 2.

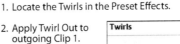

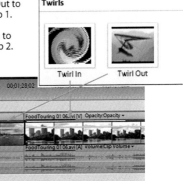

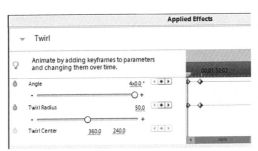

Presets are merely Premiere Elements effects to which settings and/or keyframing has already been applied. Twirl In, for instance, is keyframed from a 4x twirl to a zero twirl, using the Twirl effect to create a transition into a clip.

There is nothing particularly magical or mysterious about **Presets**. They are merely standard Premiere Elements effects to which keyframed animation have been applied to vary the effect's setting or intensity (as we do **Chapter 5, Cool Keyframing Tricks**). You can even keyframe virtually any effect to create your own custom transition. And, if you'd like, you can save it as a custom, permanent **My Preset**, as described in the *Hot Tip* below.

HOT TIP
Create Your Own Preset

If you've customized or keyframed an animated effect (as we did in **Chapter 5, Cool Keyframing Tricks**) and you'd like to save it so that you can reuse it later, you can do so simply by saving it as a **My Preset**.

To save your preset, **right-click** on the effect's listing in your clip's **Applied Effects** panel and select the option to **Save Preset**. When you save a preset, you'll have the option of setting it to attach to the beginning or end of a clip so that it can be used as a transition.

Once you've saved your preset, you can be access it by selecting the **My Presets** category of **Video Effects.**

COOL TRICK

18 Dissolve from Black & White to Color

In *Cool Trick 14*, we showed you how to use keyframing to create a transition from a modern-looking video clip into the old film effect, complete with faded color, blotches and sprocket hole damage.

The **Black & White** effect, however, is one of the few effects in the Premiere Elements set that doesn't have settings. It's either on or off – which means that you can't keyframe a transition into the effect.

But, with a clever combination of existing transitions and effects, we can still create a dissolve from a black & white video to a color video.

1 Split your clip

Position the **CTI** (playhead) over the spot in your clip that you'd like to serve as the center of your transition from black & white to color.

Click on the **Split Clip** (scissors) button that appears on the **CTI**, as illustrated.

Your clip will be sliced into two clips – which we'll call Clip 1 and Clip 2 – although, when you play the timeline, it will still play as if they were one continuous clip.

2 Locate the Black & White effect

Click on the **Edit** tab and then click the **Effects** button.

The **Black & White** effect is located in the **Image Control** category of **Video Effects**.

3 Apply the Black & White effect to Clip 1

Drag the **Black & White** effect from the **Effects** panel onto Clip 1, the first part of the clip we split in **Step 1**.

If your **CTI** is positioned over Clip 1 on your timeline, your **Monitor** will display the clip in black & white.

We now have a black & white video that abruptly changes to color. To make this transition a little more gradual, we'll add a dissolve between the two clips.

4 Locate the Cross Dissolve transition

Click the **Effects** button on the **Toolbar**.

The **Cross Dissolve** is located in the **Dissolve** category of **Video Transitions**.

Transition from black & white to color

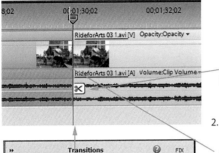

1. Position the CTI to the point on your clip that you'd like to transition from black & white to color. Click the Split Clip (scissors) button to slice the clip in two.

2. Locate the Black & White effect.

3. Apply the Black & White effect to the first part of your clip

4. Locate the Cross Dissolve transition.

5. Apply the Cross Dissolve between your two clips.

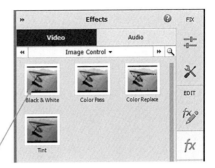

Your clip will smoothly transition from black & white to color.

5 Apply the Cross Dissolve between the clips

Drag the **Cross Dissolve** onto the place on your timeline where the two clips meet.

Because the two clips are using essentially the same visual data (except for the color information), the only effect we'll see during the transition between the two clips is the gradual addition of color to the scene.

By default, transitions last one second. If you'd like to extend this transition from black & white to color, click to select the transition on the timeline and drag on either end of it to lengthen its duration. The longer the transition, the slower the dissolve from black & white to color.

COOL TRICK

19 Rotate Your Video in Space

As we demonstrated in *Cool Trick 15, Make Your Video Tumble Through Space*, when you combine keyframing with a 3D special effect, you can create the illusion that your video is tumbling through space, toward or away from your viewer.

In this *Cool Trick*, we'll look at how to use a similar 3D effect to transition from one clip to another.

1   Locate the Camera View effect

Click the **Effects** button on the **Toolbar**.

The **Camera View** effect is located in the **Transform** category of **Video Effects**.

2   Apply the Camera View effect to Clip 1

Drag the **Camera View** effect from the **Effects** panel onto the outgoing clip (Clip 1) on your timeline.

In the **Monitor**, your video should appear slightly skewed by the default settings for the effect.

3   Apply the Camera View effect to Clip 2

Drag the same effect from the **Effects** panel onto the incoming clip (Clip 2) on your timeline.

You can also apply the same effect to several clips on the timeline by holding down the **Shift** or **Ctrl** key (the ⌘ key on a Mac) and selecting a set of clips, then dragging the effect onto any one selected clip.

HOT TIP
Precisely positioning your CTI

You can move you **CTI playhead** to very precise positions on your timeline – positioning it, for instance, to exactly one second from the end of the clip – by using the timecode to the left of the timeline's playback buttons.

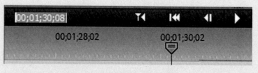

When you click to select this timecode, the numbers become dynamic, and you can overwrite them with whatever minutes, seconds or frame numbers that you'd like. When you press **Enter** after, the **CTI** playhead will jump to that precise position on your timeline!

Rotate your video in space

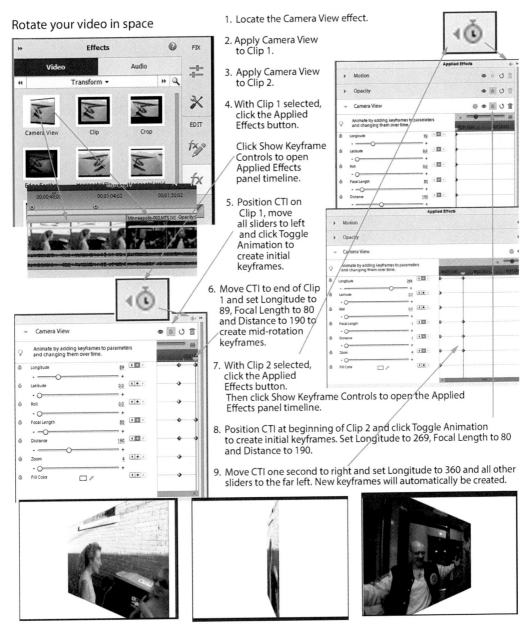

1. Locate the Camera View effect.

2. Apply Camera View to Clip 1.

3. Apply Camera View to Clip 2.

4. With Clip 1 selected, click the Applied Effects button.

   Click Show Keyframe Controls to open Applied Effects panel timeline.

5. Position CTI on Clip 1, move all sliders to left and click Toggle Animation to create initial keyframes.

6. Move CTI to end of Clip 1 and set Longitude to 89, Focal Length to 80 and Distance to 190 to create mid-rotation keyframes.

7. With Clip 2 selected, click the Applied Effects button.
   Then click Show Keyframe Controls to open the Applied Effects panel timeline.

8. Position CTI at beginning of Clip 2 and click Toggle Animation to create initial keyframes. Set Longitude to 269, Focal Length to 80 and Distance to 190.

9. Move CTI one second to right and set Longitude to 360 and all other sliders to the far left. New keyframes will automatically be created.

The effect will create a transition in which Clip 1 rotates out and then Clip 2 rotates in.

4   Open Clip 1's Applied Effects panel

With the outgoing clip selected on the timeline, click the **Applied Effects** button on the right side of the program's interface.

Click the **Camera View** listing in the **Applied Effects** panel to display the effect's settings and properties.

5 Set an initial keyframe for Clip 1's Camera View effect

Open the **Applied Effects** panel's timeline by clicking on the **Show Keyframe Controls** button (the stopwatch) in the upper right of the panel, as in the illustration on the previous page.

Position the **CTI** playhead about 1 second from the end of Clip 1.

Click the **Toggle Animation** button (the stopwatch) to the right of the **Camera View** listing. A set of keyframes points will be created for the properties of the **Camera View** effect.

Set all of the sliders to the far left so that **Longitude**, **Latitude** and **Roll** are set to zero, **Focal Length** and **Distance** are set to 1 and **Zoom** is set to 4. The video displayed in your **Monitor** should show *no* **Camera View** effects.

These settings will become your initial keyframes, and all video prior to this keyframe will look as if no **Camera View** effects have been applied to the clip.

6 Set a second keyframe for Clip 1's Camera View effect

Move the **CTI** to the end of Clip 1 and change the following **Camera View** settings:

> Set **Longitude** to 89.
> Set **Focal Length** to 80.
> Set **Distance** to 190.

New keyframe points will automatically be created at the position of the **CTI**.

These settings will collapse your video while skewing it to create the illusion of depth. In other words, it will make it appear as though your video has turned sideways inside your video frame.

If you'd like, you can also change the color of the background. To do so, click the color swatch to the right of the **Fill Color** listing and, from the **Color Picker** panel that opens, select a new background color by adjusting the Hue slider (the vertical rainbow slider in the center in the center of the panel) and then clicking on a color on the gradient window that appears on the left side of the panel.

You may want to note the R, G and B values listed for this new color in the **Color Picker** so that you can use the same color for a background in Clip 2.

7 Open Clips 2's Applied Effects panel

With the second or incoming clip selected on the timeline, click the **Applied Effects** button, if necessary, to open the **Applied Effects** panel for this clip.

Click the **Camera View** listing in the **Applied Effects** panel to display the effect's settings and properties.

8   **Set an initial keyframe for Clip 2's Camera View effect**

To complete your transition and "un-rotate" from the rotation you set up in **Step 6**, start with Clip 2 in what is essentially Clip 1's closing position and then go out to a "no effect" setting – essentially reversing the keyframes we created for Clip 1.

Open the **Applied Effects** panel's timeline by clicking on the **Show Keyframe Controls** button in the upper right of the panel, as in the illustration on the previous page.

Move the **CTI** to the beginning of Clip 2 and change the following **Camera View** settings:

Set **Longitude** to 269.
Set **Focal Length** to 80.
Set **Distance** to 190.

Click the **Toggle Animation** button (the stopwatch) to the right of the **Camera View** listing. A set of keyframes will be created for the properties of the **Camera View** effect.

If you've changed the **Fill Color** in Clip 1, you should match that color in Clip 2 so that the transition between them will be seamless.

You may notice that this clip's initial keyframe setting for **Longitude** is 269 while the previous clip's final keyframe setting for **Longitude** is 89. Using these numbers will cause our animation to rotate in from one side and out from the other.

In other words, in the animation created by this keyframing, Clip 1 will appear to swing away to the right while Clip 2 will appear to turn to swing back toward us from the left – creating a complimentary animation so that your clips seem to swing completely around in a 180-degree arc as they transition.

It's an effect that's a bit hard to describe but, if you experiment a little, using 89 rather than 269 for this keyframe's **Longitude**, you'll quickly see the difference in the animation.

9   **Set a second keyframe for Clip 2's Basic 3D effect**

Move the **CTI** to one second into Clip 2 and move all of the sliders to the far left so that **Latitude** and **Roll** are set to zero, **Focal Length** and **Distance** are set to 1 and **Zoom** is set to 4.

Set **Longitude** to 360.

Once again we're playing with numbers to create the effect we want. The 360 degree setting for **Longitude** will look exactly the same as the zero degree setting – as if no **Longitude** effect has been applied. (This is because, of course, a circle has 360 degrees, and so a 360 here gets us back to zero.)

By using 360 for this keyframe rather than zero, however, we will cause the video to complete a quarter turn in space *to the right* from 269 rather than making a three-quarter rotating backwards *to the left* to zero.

At this final keyframe position, the video displayed in your **Monitor** should show no **Camera View** effects, indicating the end of our transitional animation.

A new set of keyframes will have been automatically be created at the position of the **CTI**, and all video following this keyframe will show no **Camera View** effects applied.

When you play your video, Clip 1 should play normally until about 1 second before it ends. It should then rotate away from the camera and, when it rotates back in, it should display Clip 2.

COOL TRICK

20 Create a Custom Gradient Wipe

The **Gradient Wipe** is a uniquely customizable transition.

By design, this transition will create a wipe, from one clip to another, by following any pattern you provide it – from this pattern's blackest black point to its whitest white point.

You can create your own custom gradient pattern for this *Cool Trick*. We've also got a nice variety pack of black-to-white gradients available as a free download from Muvipix.com. Just go to our home page and do a product search on "Gradient."

Save your gradient pattern or image file to your hard drive in almost any graphics format (PSD, JPEG, TIF, etc.). When you're ready to apply it as your **Gradient Wipe**, you'll just browse to it.

1 **Locate the Gradient Wipe transition**

Click the **Transitions** button on the **Toolbar**.

The **Gradient Wipe** effect is located in the **Wipe** category of **Video Transitions**.

2 **Apply the Gradient Wipe to your clips**

Apply the **Gradient Wipe** by dragging it onto the intersection of two clips on your timeline.

Create a Custom Gradient Wipe

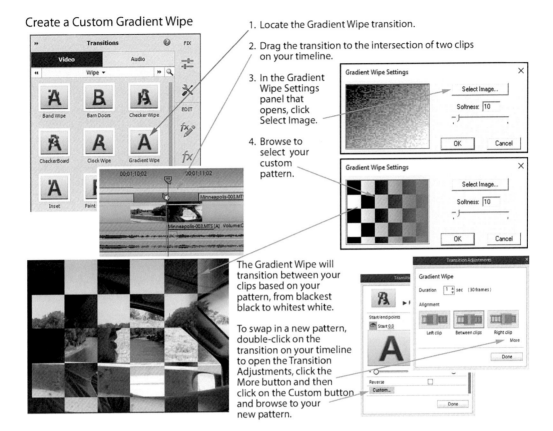

1. Locate the Gradient Wipe transition.

2. Drag the transition to the intersection of two clips on your timeline.

3. In the Gradient Wipe Settings panel that opens, click Select Image.

4. Browse to select your custom pattern.

The Gradient Wipe will transition between your clips based on your pattern, from blackest black to whitest white.

To swap in a new pattern, double-click on the transition on your timeline to open the Transition Adjustments, click the More button and then click on the Custom button and browse to your new pattern.

When you apply this transition, the **Gradient Wipe Settings** panel will automatically open.

3   Select a Gradient Wipe image

Click on the **Select Image** button on the **Gradient Wipe Settings** panel.

A Windows Explorer or Finder browse screen will open.

4   Browse to a pattern

Browse to select your gradient pattern.

Although the **Gradient Wipe** will work with virtually any image of any color combination, when you custom-create your own pattern, you'll most likely be working in grayscale – a black & white image with shades of gray.

Whatever pattern or image you choose, the **Gradient Wipe** will create its wipe transition following the image's color, from its blackest black point to its whitest white, as in the checkerboard pattern illustrated above.

Once you've selected a pattern and clicked **Open**, the image will appear in your **Gradient Wipe Settings** panel, as in the illustration on the previous page.

If you'd like, you can also adjust the **Softness** of the wipe. The "harder" you set the wipe (in other words, the lower the **Softness** setting), the more the **Gradient Wipe** will create a hard line between the old and new clip during the transition.

Click **OK**.

As you play back your video, your clips will transition from one to another based on the pattern you've provided and at the **Softness** level you've set.

As with any transition, you can slow the speed of the transition by dragging either end to extend its length on your timeline.

If you'd like to swap in a different gradient pattern at any point, double-click on the transition on your timeline and, in the **Transition Adjustments** panel that opens, click **More**, then the **Custom** button. This will re-open the **Gradient Wipe Settings** panel so that you can browse to select a new gradient for your wipe.

HOT TIP
How transitions work

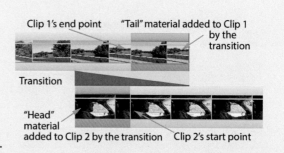

Clip 1's end point   "Tail" material added to Clip 1 by the transition

Transition

"Head" material added to Clip 2 by the transition   Clip 2's start point

Sometimes transitions seem to work in strange ways – loading unevenly between clips or re-adding frames that have been trimmed away. But knowing how they work can help you understand why they do what they do.

When you add a transition between two clips, the program needs about half a second or more of additional frames beyond each clip's end or start point to use as a **transitional footage,** the brief segment in which one clip transitions into the other. These additional frames are officially called "head" and "tail" material, and the program automatically adds them as needed.

Sometimes this means that frames you've trimmed away are re-added to your video, while other times it means that the program will create a freeze frame (when no head or tail material is available) for the transitional frames. If this happens, or if you can't seem to make your transition sit evenly on two adjacent clips, the easiest solution is to trim back your clip(s) a half a second so that the program has the additional footage it needs to create its transition.

Chapter 7
Cool Video Grid Tricks
Tricks with tracks

There are a lot of cool effects you can create when you stack your video clips on tracks, one above another.

By stacking, resizing and even skewing your clips, you can show more than one clip on-screen at once – creating a Picture-in-Picture effect or a *Brady Bunch* style tic tac toe grid of headshots!

Premiere Elements can work with as many as 99 tracks of video and 99 tracks of audio. (Possibly even more, if your computer can handle them.)

When you stack your clips on top of one another and then shape and resize them, you can show more than one clip on-screen at once – creating a split screen effect.

Skew them a bit in 3D space and two clips of talking heads seem to be talking to each other.

When you add several tracks of video and size and position them into a pattern (commonly called a grid) you can dazzle your audience with something we at Muvipix call "The Brady Bunch effect."

Combine a photo layout with some video and a little keyframing razzle dazzle and suddenly a picture in a photo album page seems to come to life on the page!

COOL TRICK

21 Do a Basic Split Screen

A split screen is, pretty simply, two or more videos appearing on screen at the same time. You create a split screen effect by stacking your videos on tracks above one another, and then resizing or cropping them so that both or all of the videos can be seen at once.

These videos can be used to create a video collage – an opening titles sequence, for instance, showing many scenes at once – or they can tell the same story from many simultaneous points of view, as in the *Oceans 11* movies.

1 Place Clip 1 on Video 1

Drag a video clip (Clip 1) from the **Project Assets** panel to the Video 1 track on your timeline.

HOT TIP
Adding video and audio tracks

When you open a new project, the timeline will display Voice, Music and one or two video and audio tracks by default. There are three ways to add audio and video tracks to your timeline:

1 **Right-click** on an empty space on an existing track on the timeline and select the option to **Add Tracks**;

2 Drag an audio or video clip to a blank spot on the timeline above an existing video track. When you release your mouse button, a new video/audio track set will automatically be created and your clip will be added to it.

3 Select the **Add Tracks** option from the **Timeline** menu at the top of the program's interface.

Do a Basic Split Screen

1. Place Clip 1 on the Video 1 track.

2. Place Clip 2 on the Video 2 track.

3. Click to select Clip 2 on the timeline and then click Applied Effects.

4. In the Motion properties, set Clip 2's Position to 210 145 and Scale to 55%.

5. Click to select Clip 1 on the timeline and then click Applied Effects.

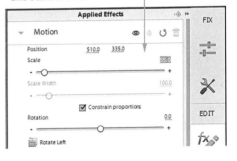

6. In the Motion properties, set Clip 1's Position to 510 355 and Scale to 55%.

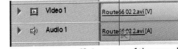

2   Place Clip 2 on Video 2

Drag a second video clip (Clip 2) from the **Project Assets** panel to the Video 2 track on your timeline, directly above Clip 1, as in the illustration above.

If your project doesn't yet have a Video 2 track, drag your clip to the blank space right above Clip 1. When you release the mouse button, a new video track will automatically be created and Clip 2 will appear in it.

You can continue to add videos on new tracks in the same manner as in **Step 2**. Premiere Elements is capable of working with as many as 99 tracks of video and/or audio. The more tracks you add, however, the more power and RAM space the program will demand from your computer.

Audio and video tracks can be opened and fully displayed or displayed as compressed tracks by clicking the triangle-shaped toggle to the left of each track header.

To make more efficient use of the panel's vertical space, individual tracks on the Timeline can be toggled between a compressed and an open view.

When working with several tracks of video, you may need to scroll up, using the scroll bar at the far right of the **Timeline** panel, to see all of your tracks of video.

You can also click and drag on the seams between the panels in the Premiere Elements interface and resize your **Monitor** panel temporarily smaller so that you can see all of your audio and video tracks.

To squeeze more timeline into less space, you can right-click on a blank space on your timeline and select the **Track Size** option. You can also uncheck **Audio Tracks** on this menu so that only your video tracks are displayed, buying you a bit more vertical space.

3   **Open Clip 2's Applied Effects panel**

With Clip 2 (the upper clip) selected on the timeline, click the **Applied Effects** button on the right side of the interface.

Click on the **Motion** effect listing on the **Applied Effects** panel to open its properties and settings.

4   **Resize and reposition Clip 2**

Set Clip 2's **Scale** to 55%.
Set Clip 2's **Position** to 210 145. (For high-def, use 585 340.)

Clip 2 video will be about half its normal size and will appear in the upper left of your video frame in the **Monitor** panel. Clip 1 will be partially visible "under" it.

5   **Open Clip 1's Applied Effects panel**

With Clip 1 (the lower clip) selected on the timeline, click the **Applied Effects** button on the right side of the interface.

Click on the **Motion** effect listing on the **Applied Effects** panel to open its properties and settings.

6   **Resize and reposition Clip 1**

Set Clip 1's **Scale** to 55%
Set Clip 1's **Position** to 510 335. (For high-def, use 1315 710.)

Clip 1 will appear, at roughly half its size, in the lower right of your video frame.

Even if this isn't the final position you want your clips to be in, this is a good starting point for a split screen effect.

With both clips visible in the **Monitor,** you can now reposition them to anywhere in your video frame just by clicking on them and dragging them new positions in the **Monitor** panel.

Also, if you click to select a clip in the **Monitor**, corner handles will appear on the clip. By dragging these corners in or out, you can change the clip's **Scale**.

Using the same basic process, you can add, size and position almost any number of clips to your split screen video frame.

And, if you add a color or other background to your Video 1 track rather than a clip and stack your video on tracks above it, your split screen clips will have an interesting background to float over.

And finally, of course, using keyframing, you can animate your split screen clips to change scale and position over time so that, say, you can zoom out from a single clip to a split screen or zoom in one clip so that it fills your video frame.

COOL TRICK

22 Create a "Nightline" 3D Split Screen

"Nightline" was a terrific late-night news and interview show that ran on ABC for over 30 years. One of its often-imitated features is the live remote panel discussion, in which two or more people, in different locations, comment on a situation and respond to each other via video link-up. Although these people are often separated by hundreds or even thousands of miles, they are able to address each other via the video link, often appearing on TV in split-screen, as if they are all in the same room.

To add to the illusion that these people are actually speaking to each other, the program would sometimes tilt and skew each of their video images in 3D space so that they seemed to be facing one another.

In this *Cool Trick*, we'll show you how to apply a simple 3D move to your split screen to accomplish a similar effect.

1 **Place Clip 1 on Video 1**

   Drag a video clip (Clip 1) from your **Project Assets** panel to the Video 1 track on your timeline.

2 **Place Clip 2 on Video 2**

   Drag a second video clip (Clip 2) from the **Project Assets** panel to the Video 2 track on your timeline, directly above Clip 1, as in the illustration on the following page.

   If your project doesn't yet have a Video 2 track, drag your clip to the blank space right above Clip 1. When you release the mouse button, a new video track will automatically be created and Clip 2 will appear on it.

Create a "Nightline" 3D Split Screen

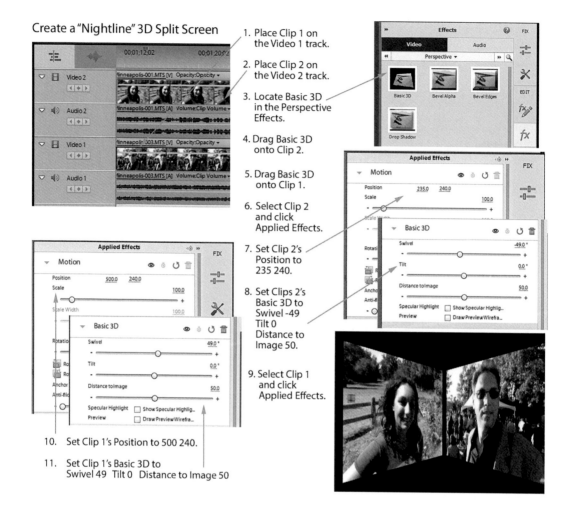

1. Place Clip 1 on the Video 1 track.

2. Place Clip 2 on the Video 2 track.

3. Locate Basic 3D in the Perspective Effects.

4. Drag Basic 3D onto Clip 2.

5. Drag Basic 3D onto Clip 1.

6. Select Clip 2 and click Applied Effects.

7. Set Clip 2's Position to 235 240.

8. Set Clips 2's Basic 3D to Swivel -49 Tilt 0 Distance to Image 50.

9. Select Clip 1 and click Applied Effects.

10. Set Clip 1's Position to 500 240.

11. Set Clip 1's Basic 3D to Swivel 49   Tilt 0   Distance to Image 50

3   Locate the Basic 3D effect

Click the **Effects** button on the **Toolbar**.

The **Basic 3D** effect is located in the **Perspective** category of **Video Effects**.

4   Apply the Basic 3D effect to Clip 1

Drag the **Basic 3D** effect from the **Effects** panel onto Clip 1 on your timeline.

5   Apply the Basic 3D effect to Clip 2

Drag the **Basic 3D** effect from the **Effects** panel onto Clip 2 on your timeline.

6   Open Clip 2's Applied Effects panel

With the Clip 2 (the upper clip) selected on the timeline, click the **Applied Effects** button on the right side of the interface.

7   Reposition Clip 2

Click on the **Motion** effect listing on the **Applied Effects** panel to open its properties and settings.

Set Clip 2's **Position** to 235 240. (For high-def, use 600 540.)

Clip 2 will move one-third of the way left in your video frame.

8   Set Basic 3D for Clip 2

Click on the **Basic 3D** effect listing on the **Applied Effects** panel to open its properties and settings.

Set **Swivel** to -49 degrees.
Set **Tilt** to 0 degrees.
Set **Distance to Image** to 50.

Clip 2 will appear in the left half of your video frame, angled as if facing to the right.

9   Open Clip 1's Applied Effects panel

With Clip 1 (the lower clip) selected on the timeline, click the **Applied Effects** button on the right side of the interface.

10   Reposition Clip 1

Click on the **Motion** effect listing on the **Applied Effects** panel to open its properties and settings.

Set Clip 1's **Position** to 500 245. (For high-def, use 1305 540.)

Clip 1 will move one-third of the way right in your video frame.

11   Set Basic 3D for Clip 1

Click on the **Basic 3D** effect listing on the **Applied Effects** panel to open its properties and settings.

Set **Swivel** to 49 degrees.
Set **Tilt** to 0 degrees.
Set **Distance to Image** to 50.

Clip 1 will appear in the right half of your video frame, angled as if facing to the left.

Because we've swiveled Clip 2 49 degrees and Clip 1 -49 degrees, the two clips will appear in your video frame to be facing each other in 3D space.

With nothing on a video track below them, these clips seem to be floating over blackness. You can, of course, add a bit more interest by moving these clips each up one track (move Clip 2 to Video 3 and Clip 1 to Video 2). You can then place a motion background or even just a color clip on Video 1 to create a backdrop for your split screen discussion.

23 Create a "Brady Bunch" Video Grid

The steps we'll use to create the "Brady Bunch" grid effect are not that much different than the steps used to create a basic split screen, as we did in *Cool Trick 21*. They're just more-so.

In other words, with the "Brady Bunch" grid (so named because it's based on the tic tac toe-style collage of video clips that opened the classic TV sit-com), rather than *two* clips sharing the same video frame, *nine* clips will share the screen space.

In my version of the *Cool Trick*, I'm adding yet another layer – a template that I'll place on the Video 1 track so that I can line up my other video clips.

About the biggest challenge with this *Cool Trick* is that it uses 10 tracks of video – which means that your timeline will take up a lot of vertical space.

There are a couple of ways you can work with this increased vertical space:

- You can keep the tracks closed or arrange the sizes of the panels in the Premiere Elements interface to give your timeline more room;

- If your computer has two monitors, you can select the **Dual Monitor Workspace** option under the program's **Window** menu – which separates the timeline from the rest of the interface – and drag the timeline to your second monitor so that it has an entire screen to itself;

- Or you can just leave the interface as is and just do a lot of a scrolling up and down of the timeline as you work.

It might also help to right-click on a blank area of the timeline and, in the context menu, uncheck **Audio Tracks**.

In this mode (as in my illustration on the following page) your timeline will display only your video tracks – which can save a bit of vertical space on your timeline.

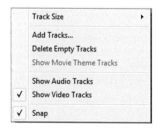

Create a "Brady Bunch" Video Grid

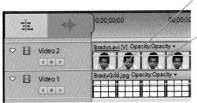

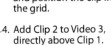

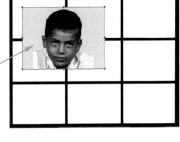

1. Place your grid pattern on Video 1.

2. Add Clip 1 to Video 2, directly above the pattern.

3. Click on the clip in the Monitor and, by dragging the corner handles, scale and position the clip in the grid.

4. Add Clip 2 to Video 3, directly above Clip 1.

5. Click on the clip in the Monitor and, by dragging the corner handles, scale and position the clip in the grid.

6. Repeat this pattern, adding clips above one another and scaling and positioning each in the grid.

1   **Place your grid pattern on Video 1**

This is optional, of course. But, if you've got a complicated pattern of images, temporarily placing a grid or pattern on the Video 1 track can help you line it all up. (You can later delete this pattern from your timeline, if you'd like.)

For this "Brady Bunch" effect, you can create your own grid or download my file free BradyGrid.jpg or BradyGridHighDef.jpg image from the products page at Muvipix.com.

HOT TIP
Scale and Position

The **Scale** and **Position** properties are measurements of the size and location of a clip in your video frame.

Scale, measured in percentage, is the size of your clip, as displayed in the video frame.

Position is a set of vector coordinates, measured in pixels, from the top left of your video frame. For instance, in an NTSC 720x480 pixel video frame, the center position of the frame is 360 240. In the PAL video system, the center of a 720x576 pixel video frame is 360 288.

The center of a 1920x1080 high-definition video frame is 960 540.

2   **Place Clip 1 on Video 2**

Although this *Cool Trick* has many steps, its steps are all executed pretty similarly – so you'll essentially repeat **Step 2** and **Step 3** for each clip.

And once you get the pattern going – placing a clip and then scaling and positioning it in the grid – you'll see that it's not as complicated as it might at first seem.

Drag a video clip (Clip 1) from your **Project Assets** panel to the Video 2 track on your timeline, directly above the grid. (You can drag one end of the grid to extend it so that it's the same length as Clip 1, if you'd like.)

3   **Scale and position Clip 1 into your grid**

The easiest and most intuitive way to scale and position a clip is to do it right on the **Monitor** panel.

When you click on a clip displayed in the **Monitor**, corner handles will appear around it.

By dragging the corner handles in and out, you can increase or decrease the scale, or size, of your video clip. By clicking and dragging on the clip itself, you can position it in your video frame.

If you'd prefer, you can set the clip's **Scale** and **Position** numerically instead. To do this, make sure the clip is selected on your timeline and click the **Applied Effects** button. In the **Applied Effects** panel that opens, click on the **Motion** listing to display its settings and properties.

To fit my BradyGrid.jpg, use the following settings for the first square of the grid if you're working in standard definition:

Set **Position** to 125 80
Set **Scale** to 31%

To fit the high-definition version, BradyGridHighDef.jpg, use the following settings for the first square of the grid:

Set **Position** to 330 185
Set **Scale** to 31%

4   Place Clip 2 on Video 3

Drag a second video clip (Clip 2) from the **Project Assets** panel to the Video 3 track on your timeline, directly above Clip 1, as in the illustration on the previous page.

If your project doesn't yet have a Video 2 track, drag your clip to the blank space right above Clip 1. When you release the mouse button, a new video track will automatically be created and your clip will appear on it.

5   Scale and Position Clip 2 over your grid

As in **Step 3**, you can click and drag on your clip or its corner handles to position and scale it in the grid.

6   Repeat this pattern with all of your clips

If you'd like to set their positions numerically (so that your clips precisely line up), you can use the following positions.

To fit my BradyGrid, you'll **Scale** all of your video clips to 31%.

Clip 1	**Clip 2**	**Clip 3**
Position 125 80	Position 360 80	Position 595 80
Clip 4	**Clip 5**	**Clip 6**
Position 125 240	Position 360 240	Position 595 240
Clip 7	**Clip 8**	**Clip 9**
Position 125 400	Position 360 400	Position 595 400

For high-definition video, again **Scale** all video clips to 31% and use these **Position** numbers:

Clip 1	**Clip 2**	**Clip 3**
Position 330 185	Position 720 185	Position 1590 185
Clip 4	**Clip 5**	**Clip 6**
Position 330 540	Position 960 540	Position 1590 540
Clip 7	**Clip 8**	**Clip 9**
Position 330 900	Position 960 900	Position 1590 900

24 Go to a Video from a Still Photo Composition

This is a fun effect that creates the illusion that a photo album (or any other photo composition you've created) has suddenly come to life – one of its pictures leaping off the page and becoming a living video!

You'll need a dummy photo album page to make it work. (In my case, I just photographed a page of my photo album to use as my background.)

We'll also create a "freeze frame" of the first frame of our video and position it so that, at the beginning of the effect, it appears to be one of the photos on the page.

1   **Place Clip 1 on Video 1**

The first thing we'll need to do is create a freeze frame of the first frame of our video.

This will serve as a photo in our photo album – before it comes to life as a video. Because of the way Premiere Elements creates freeze frames, we'll need to do this on Video 1 and then move it and our video up to Video 2.

Place your video clip on the Video 1 track.

2   **Make a Freeze Frame**

Press the **Home** button on your keyboard so that the **CTI** playhead is positioned on the first frame of your video.

Click the **Tools** button on the Premiere Elements **Toolbar** and select **Freeze Frame.**

When the **Freeze Frame** option panel appears, click the **Insert in Movie** button.

A 5-second still photo of your video's first frame will appear on your timeline at the position of the **CTI**, moving your video to the right to make room for it.

(If this insert action leaves a frame or two of your video to the left of your freeze frame on your timeline, select and delete it. You want to ensure that the freeze frame is the first clip in your movie.)

3   **Move the Freeze Frame and clip to Video 2**

Drag the freeze frame and the video clip up to the Video 2 track. This will free up the Video 1 track so we can place our photo album background behind your video.

Go to a Video from a Still Photo Composition

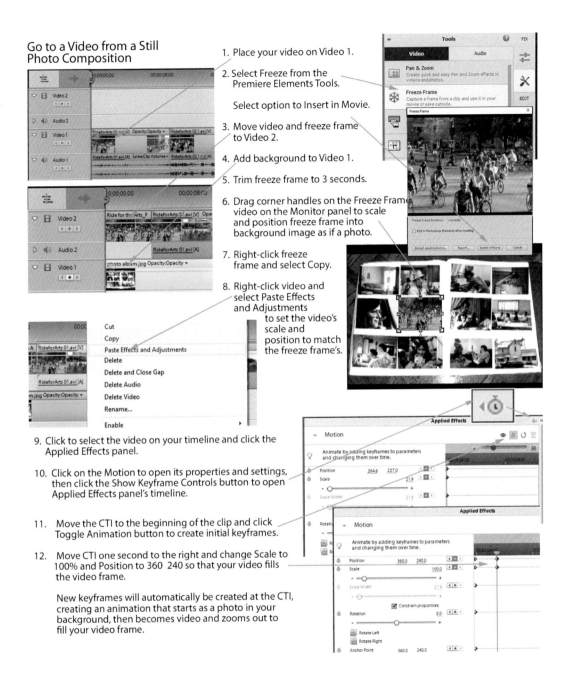

1. Place your video on Video 1.

2. Select Freeze from the Premiere Elements Tools.

   Select option to Insert in Movie.

3. Move video and freeze frame to Video 2.

4. Add background to Video 1.

5. Trim freeze frame to 3 seconds.

6. Drag corner handles on the Freeze Frame video on the Monitor panel to scale and position freeze frame into background image as if a photo.

7. Right-click freeze frame and select Copy.

8. Right-click video and select Paste Effects and Adjustments to set the video's scale and position to match the freeze frame's.

9. Click to select the video on your timeline and click the Applied Effects panel.

10. Click on the Motion to open its properties and settings, then click the Show Keyframe Controls button to open Applied Effects panel's timeline.

11. Move the CTI to the beginning of the clip and click Toggle Animation button to create initial keyframes.

12. Move CTI one second to the right and change Scale to 100% and Position to 360 240 so that your video fills the video frame.

    New keyframes will automatically be created at the CTI, creating an animation that starts as a photo in your background, then becomes video and zooms out to fill your video frame.

4   Add the background image to Video 1

Drag the image you plan to use for your background – in my case, a picture of my photo album – to the Video 1 track, directly below your other clips. This clip will be the default image length of 5 seconds, the same duration as your freeze frame. (Note that, because the freeze frame is currently filling the video frame, your background will not yet be visible in the **Monitor**.)

5   Trim the freeze frame

Click to select the freeze frame on the timeline and, by clicking and dragging on its end, trim the duration of the freeze frame to about 3 seconds.

The video clip to the right might ripple left to fill in the gap. If it does not, manually drag it up against the freeze frame.

6   Scale and position the freeze frame

Click on the freeze frame in the **Monitor** panel. When you click on it, corner handles will appear around it.

By dragging these corner handles inward, you can reduce the freeze frame's size or **Scale**.

To reposition the freeze frame, click on it in the **Monitor** and drag it to where you'd like it appear.

Scale and position your freeze frame so that it seems to be a part of your background image. In my case, I've positioned my freeze frame so that it appears to be a photo in my photo album.

7   Copy the freeze frame's scale and position

In order to duplicate the current scale and position settings for our freeze frame and apply them to our video clip, we'll use the **Paste Effects and Adjustments** feature.

Right-click on the freeze frame on the timeline and select **Copy**.

8   Paste Attributes to the video

Right-click on your video clip on the timeline and select the option to **Paste Effects and Adjustments**.

This feature will paste any properties, settings or animations from one clip to one or more others – in this case copying the **Position** and **Scale** of the freeze frame onto the video clip. Because the **Scale** and **Position** for the video and the freeze frame are identical, when we play the timeline, the freeze frame will now seamlessly blend into your video.

Now that we've created an effect in which a still photo suddenly becomes a moving video, we'll use keyframing to create an animation so that your video appears to fly out of the background and fill the video frame.

9   Open the video clip's Applied Effects panel

With the video selected on your timeline, click the **Applied Effects** button on the right side of the interface.

10 **Open Motion's Keyframe Controls**

The **Applied Effects** panel will open.

Click on the **Motion** listing to open its properties and settings.

Click the **Show Keyframe Controls** button (the stopwatch) in the upper right of the panel to open the **Applied Effects** panel timeline, as illustrated on page 93.

11 **Create initial keyframes for Motion**

Position the **CTI** on the **Applied Effects** panel timeline at the beginning of the video clip.

Click the **Toggle Animation** button.

A set of keyframe points will be created at the position of the **CTI** on the **Applied** panel timeline.

12 **Create a second set of keyframes**

Move the **CTI** about one or two seconds to the right on the **Applied Effects** panel timeline.

Change **Scale** to 100%.
Change **Position** to 360 240, the center of the video frame. (If you are using PAL video, change the **Position** to 360 288. And, if you are working in high-definition video, set the **Position** to 960 540.)

A new set of keyframe points will automatically be created at the position of the **CTI** for **Scale** and **Position**.

When we play the completed video, it will begin with the photo album.

Then, about 3 seconds in, that one of the photos will come to life – flying right off the page and becoming a moving video as it grows to fill the video frame!

There are a number of interesting variations available for this effect.

- You can keep the video the same size as the freeze frame and just have it play as if the photo came to life on the photo album page.

- You can add several layers of videos, properly scaled and positioned (as in *Cool Trick 23, Create a "Brady Bunch" Video Grid*) so that *all* of the photos in your photo album suddenly spring to life!

- You can even reverse the effect – so that your video suddenly freezes, shrinks and becomes a still picture in a photo album.

Chapter 8
Cool Tricks with Time
Speeding things up and slowing things down

With the tools in Premiere Elements, you can slow things down – and you can speed things up!

Time Stretch is a great, easy-to-use tool for creating slow-motion, time-lapse and even video that plays in reverse.

And the new Time Remapping tool can create video that includes several "Time Zones," each playing at a different speed!

There are a couple of ways to shift time in your movies in Premiere Elements. The **Time Stretch** tool is a simplified tool for speeding up or slowing down a clip. And the much more advanced **Time Remapping** tool lets you create a number of time shifts within a single video clip.

In *Cool Trick 25, Make a High-Speed Time Lapse Sequence*, we'll use **Time Stretch** to shift a scene into fast motion.

In *Cool Trick 26, Create a Time Warp Effect*, we'll use **Time Remapping** to vary our playback, speeding up, then suddenly slowing down a sequence.

Then, in *Cool Trick 27, Play Your Video in Reverse*, we'll show you how to set up your video clip to play backwards.

Finally, in *Cool Trick 28*, we'll show you how to use time as a special effect, using **Posterize Time** – an effect that's technically not a time stretch, but one which does create some interesting, time-based visual effects.

25 Make a High-Speed Time Lapse Sequence

You've seen the effect dozens of times: Suddenly time speeds up. The sun quickly rises and clouds rush across the sky. A flower blooms in mere seconds. Rush hour street traffic zips around in an almost choreographed dance.

In this *Cool Trick*, we'll use the **Time Stretch** tool to quadruple our clips's playback speed so that our one minute of video plays in about 15 seconds – converting a monotonous video about digging out after a snowstorm into a high-speed, very condensed look at our efforts.

Note that the **Time Stretch** tool is only available in Expert view.

1 Select a clip on your timeline

Click to select the clip on your timeline that you'd like to apply a **Time Stretch** to.

2 Select the Timeline Time Stretch tool

Right-click on a clip on your timeline and, from the **Clip** sub-menu, select **Time Stretch**.

3 Set your clip's playback speed

The **Time Stretch** option panel that opens offers you two settings for time shifting your clip: **Speed** and **Duration** (in addition to the option to play the clip in reverse.)

Make a High-Speed Time Lapse Sequence

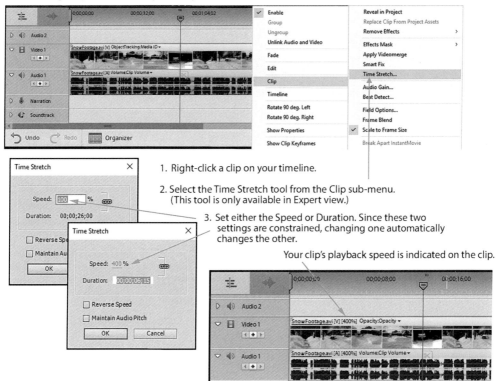

1. Right-click a clip on your timeline.

2. Select the Time Stretch tool from the Clip sub-menu. (This tool is only available in Expert view.)

3. Set either the Speed or Duration. Since these two settings are constrained, changing one automatically changes the other.

Your clip's playback speed is indicated on the clip.

By default, these two settings are constrained. In other words, changing **Speed** automatically changes **Duration**; and changing **Duration** naturally changes playback **Speed**. If you set the clip's playback speed to 200%, the clip's duration will be half as long. If you set the clip's playback speed to 50%, it will be twice as long.

By clicking to break the chain link that connects these two settings on the **Time Stretch** panel, you can unconstrain them. This would be useful if, for instance, you wanted to keep your clip the same length (say it was already placed in your movie) but you wanted it to play in slow motion.

In this case, the **Time Stretch** tool will slow down your clip – but will cut it when it reaches the duration you've designated (even if the entire clip has not played).

So what happens if you've got a one-minute clip and you set it to play twice as fast and remain the same duration? In this case, the clip will be *forced to* abbreviate its duration, since it will run out of footage.

On **Time Stretch** option screen, click to select the **Speed** number and type in 400%. When you click **OK**, the clip will play back at 4x speed.

26 Create a Time Warp Effect

This trendy little special effect has been used so often in movies and on TV shows lately that it's almost become a cliché. Still, it *is* an attention-getter!

In the "time warp" effect, your video will start out playing at regular speed, then suddenly ramp up to quadruple speed for a few seconds, then drop back to normal speed – or even slow motion. (If you were editing a TV show with this effect, you might even accompany this sudden speed-up with a "whoosh" sound, just to emphasize the sudden shift in time.)

If you aren't familiar with the effect, all you need to do is watch an evening of prime time TV. Every show from reality TV to "CSI" to virtually every action movie made in the past 10 years uses it for their transitional sequences. It's often used to make an establishing shot of the outside of a building more interesting, and it's usually accompanied by a zoom – so that the video starts as a slow zoom, then suddenly speeds up, then slows down again.

In our exercise, we'll start at normal speed, then speed up, then go to slow motion, then back to normal again.

Fortunately, Premiere Elements' new **Time Remapping** tool makes doing this kind of video wizardry simple!

1 **Select a clip on your timeline**

You'll want a scene that runs at least 30 seconds or so.

2 **Open the Time Remapping workspace**

Click the **Tools** button on the **Toolbar**, along the bottom of the program. Select **Time Remapping** from the **Video Tools**.

The **Time Remapping** workspace will open, as illustrated.

3 **Create a Time Zone**

A **Time Zone** is the portion of your clip you designate for the **Time Remapping** effect. Different playback speeds can be set for each **Time Zone** you create.

Create a **Time Zone** by clicking the **Create Time Zone** button or by simply clicking the **+** button on the **CTI** playhead.

4 **Size and position your Time Zone**

Drag on either end of your **Time Zone** to lengthen it and position it over the segment you want the effect applied to.

In the lower right of the workspace you'll also find options for setting **Ease In** and **Ease Out**. Checking these options will cause playback to ramp up or ramp down to the speed you've set for your **Time Zone** rather than change speed abruptly.

Create a Time Warp Effect

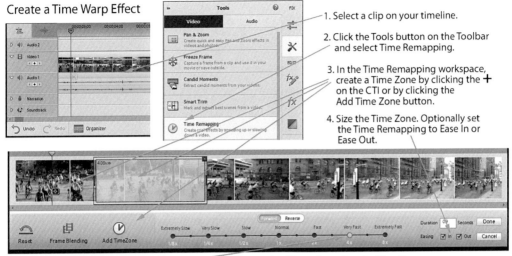

1. Select a clip on your timeline.

2. Click the Tools button on the Toolbar and select Time Remapping.

3. In the Time Remapping workspace, create a Time Zone by clicking the + on the CTI or by clicking the Add Time Zone button.

4. Size the Time Zone. Optionally set the Time Remapping to Ease In or Ease Out.

5. With a Time Zone selected, set a playback speed. This speed will be indicated on the Time Zone.

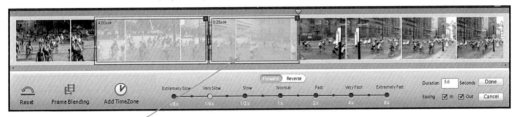

6. Create and set additional Time Zones.

5   Set your Time Zone's playback speed

The **Time Zone's** playback speed is set by a very intuitive slider. The playback speed of your **Time Zone** is also indicated on the upper left corner of the **Time Zone** itself.

The **Duration** of your **Time Zone** is indicated in the lower right of the workspace. This **Duration** will, of course, change as you change your playback speed. As an alternative to setting the playback speed with the slider, you can type in a **Duration** for your **Time Zone** and the program will automatically set the playback speed.

It's important to note that this **Duration** represents the duration of the **Time Zone** you currently have selected only. It is not the **Duration** of your entire clip. This indicator can be very helpful, then, if you're trying to create a number **of Time Zones**, each of which runs at its own playback speed but each of which you want to keep the same duration.

6   Create additional Time Zones

In our exercise, illustrated above, we've created two **Time Zones**, following up our 4x speed-up with a shift to slow-motion at one-fourth speed.

A clip can include as many **Time Zones** as you'd like, each shifting into its own specific playback speed.

Play Your Video in Reverse

1. Right-click on a clip on your timeline.

2. Select Time Stretch from the Clip sub-menu.

3. In the Time Stretch option panel, check Reverse Speed.

4. If you'd like, you can also change playback speed.

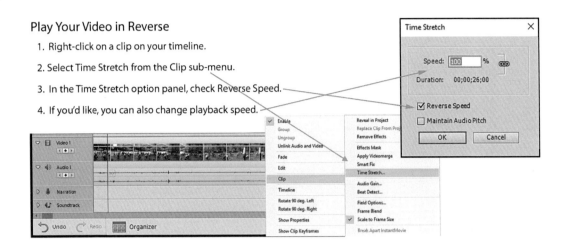

27 Play Your Video in Reverse

It's always kind of fun to play a video clip backwards. A high diver flying backwards out of a pool and landing on a diving board. A person walking backwards to his car and driving down the street in reverse. Maybe even a bride leaving her groom at the altar, linking arms with her father and backing out of the church.

Both the **Time Stretch** tool and the **Time Remapping** tool are capable of reversing playback of a clip. And, with either tool, this reverse playback can be set to play at normal speed, fast motion or slow motion.

1 Select a clip on your timeline

Ideally it will be a clip that benefits from being played backwards – either because it's funny or it defies the laws of nature (like a high diver flying out of the water and up to his diving board).

2 Open the Time Stretch panel for this clip

Right-click on a clip on your timeline and, from the **Clip** sub-menu, select **Time Stretch** .

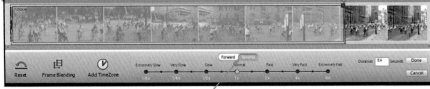

The Time Remapping tool can also be used to reverse playback of your video – however, it can look rather clumsy if only a segment of a clip is reversed.

3   Set Time Stretch to Reverse Speed

On the **Time Stretch** option panel, check **Reverse Speed**.

4   Change the Playback Speed

This is optional, of course – but you can increase the energy of a reversed clip by speeding it up (increasing the **Playback Speed** percentage) or you can make it more dramatic by slowing it down (decreasing the **Playback Speed** percentage).

COOL TRICK

28 Posterize Time

The Premiere Elements **Posterize Time** effect isn't technically a time effect. It doesn't increase your clip's playback speed or cause it to reverse, slow down or stop. In fact, although it seems to affect your clip's frame rate, it doesn't actually even change *that*!

But it is a very cool special effect. Its purpose is to create a sort of surreal look in which things don't quite move naturally. The action doesn't change playback speed – but the video is given a strobe-like effect, its motion coming in a series of slow, frozen frames rather than smoothly and naturally.

It's a great effect for creating sort of a drugged or dream-like sequence, just unreal enough to signal that something in your movie isn't quite right.

1   Locate the Old film effect

Click the **Effects** button on the **Toolbar**.

Posterize Time is in the **Time** category of **Video Effects**.

2   Apply Posterize Time to your clip

Drag the **Posterize Time** effect onto your clip on the timeline.

Posterize Time

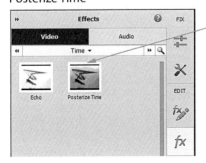

1. Locate Posterize Time in the Time category of Video Effects.

2. Drag or apply Posterize Time to your clip.

3. With the clip selected on your timeline, open the Applied Effects panel.

4. Adjust Posterize Time's Frame Rate effect.

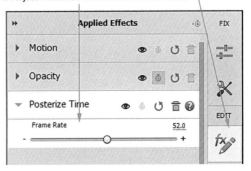

Remember, this effect will be most noticeable with motion, so choose a clip with plenty of action or camera movement.

3   **Open the clip's Applied Effects panel**

With the clip selected on your timeline, click the **Applied Effects** button on the right side of the interface.

4   **Set the Posterize Time Frame Rate**

Click on the **Posterize Time** listing on the **Applied Effects** panel to open the effect's properties and settings.

Using either the slider or by typing the number numerically, set the **Frame Rate** for the effect.

A setting of 5-10 frames per second creates a nice surreal effect.

A setting of 1 frame per second will make your clip look like a series of brief freeze frames.

Setting the effect at over 20 frames per second (which is close to a typical video's frame rate) will result in a much milder, maybe even imperceptible effect.

Chapter 9

Cool Track Matte Tricks

Cutting holes through your videos

The Track Matte is one of Premiere Elements' most powerful tools.

Using the Track Matte, you can create a transparent spot in a video – and then animate that spot so that this transparency moves around your video frame.

Matting is a way of cutting a window, or making a transparent shape, through your video. When you make an area of your video transparent, whatever is on the video track below it shows through this window.

Mattes come in many forms in Premiere Elements. The **Crop** effect, for instance, is essentially a matte tool for making the sides of your video transparent. Using the various **Garbage Mattes**, you can draw almost any shape, rendering everything outside of that shape transparent, effectively creating a custom crop in any shape you need.

The **Track Matte** is a uniquely powerful way to make areas of your video transparent. The **Track Matte** bases the location, size and shape of this transparency on a shape on a separate video track. Using keyframing, you can animate the size and position of this shape – and the **Track Matte** will follow it. In other words, using the **Track Matte**, you can follow a person or object around your video frame with almost any special effect!

By the way, don't be intimidated by the number of steps it takes to create a **Track Matte** effect. As you'll see, virtually all **Track Matte** effects use the same basic steps – creating a shape for the matte to follow, keyframing its motion around the frame and then setting the **Track Matte** to follow it. So, once you've mastered the basics, you'll be able to create virtually any **Track Matte** effect you can imagine!

HOT TIP
How the Track Matte works

The **Track Matte** is applied to a video on an upper track (Video 2, for instance).

It will then display *only the area of the video represented by the shape* placed on a video track above it (Video 3, for instance).

Everything outside that shape will become transparent – revealing whatever is on the video track below it (Video 1, for instance).

If the video on Video 1 and Video 2 is the same clip and an effect is applied to the clip on only one of the video tracks, the **Track Matte** will make it appear that the effect is applied only outside or only inside the matte area.

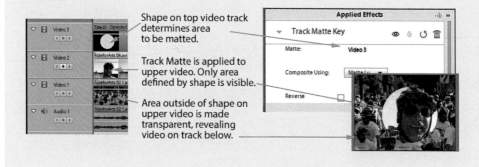

Highlight a Person in a Crowd (Part 1)

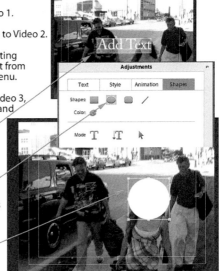

1. Add your clip to Video 1.

2. Add the identical clip to Video 2.

3. Create a title by selecting New Text/Default Text from the program's Text menu.

   Ensure your title is on Video 3, above your other clips, and is stretched to the same length.

4. Delete the placeholder text.

5. Select the Oval shape tool from the Title Adjustments Shapes tools.

6. Draw an oval over the person you want to highlight.

COOL TRICK

29 Highlight a Person in a Crowd

Okay, so you've got some great video of the entire varsity football team on the field. But there's one player in particular you'd like to highlight.

You can spotlight him, as we do in *Cool Trick 2, Spotlight an Area of Your Video*. Or, using the **Track Matte**, you can create an effect that dims everything but the person you want to highlight in the shot.

As with many **Track Matte** effects, this one uses the same video clip on both Video 1 and Video 2. But, by applying an effect to the clip on Video 1 and then using the **Track Matte** to make everything outside of a defined area transparent, we'll make it appear that we've only added an effect to the area of the video defined by our **Matte**.

1 **Place your clip on Video 1**

   Drag your clip from the **Project Assets** panel to the Video 1 track on your timeline.

2 **Place the same clip on Video 2**

   Drag the same clip from the **Project Assets** panel to the Video 2 track, directly above the first clip.

   These two clips should be identical and aligned, one above the other.

3   **Create a title above these video clips**

We will create our tracking object by drawing a shape created in Premiere Elements **Title Adjustments** workspace. You could, as an alternative, create your shape, using a program like Photoshop Elements, save it as a PSD with no background layer and import it into your Premiere Elements project.

To create a shape in the **Title Adjustments** workspace, position the **CTI** at the very beginning of your clips and then select **New Text/ Default Text** from the program's **Text** menu.

The **Title Adjustments** panel will open and the placeholder words "Add Text" will appear on the **Monitor** panel.

You may need to stop at this point and ensure that your title is in position, directly above your clips, and that it is stretched on the timeline, if necessary, so that it is the same duration as your video clips, as illustrated on the previous page. To re-open the **Title Adjustments** panel, double-click on the title.

4   **Delete the placeholder text**

When the **Default Text** title opens, use the **Title Adjustments Selection Tool** (the arrow) to select the placeholder text and then press the **Delete** key on your keyboard to remove it.

5   **Select the Oval shape tool**

Click to select the **Shapes** tab on the **Title Adjustments** panel and select the oval shape.

6   **Draw an oval over the area you want to highlight**

Drag the **Oval** shape tool to create a white oval over the person you want to highlight in your video. (To constrain this shape to a circle, hold down the **Shift** key as you drag.)

Once you've drawn the oval, you can use the **Selection Tool** and tweak its size and position.

Click on the timeline to exit the **Title Adjustments** workspace. Your timeline should now show your video clips on Video 1 and Video 2 and your white oval graphic on Video 3.

7   **Open the shape's Applied Effects panel**

The next step is to keyframe the shape's position in the video frame so that it follows the person we want to highlight throughout the clip.

Click to select the white oval clip on your timeline and click the **Applied Effects** button on the right side of the program.

8   **Open the Applied Effects panel timeline**

Click on the **Motion** listing in the **Applied Effects** panel to open its settings and properties.

Highlight a Person in a Crowd (Part 2)

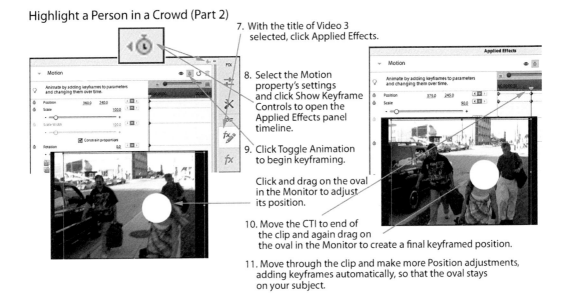

7. With the title of Video 3 selected, click Applied Effects.

8. Select the Motion property's settings and click Show Keyframe Controls to open the Applied Effects panel timeline.

9. Click Toggle Animation to begin keyframing.

Click and drag on the oval in the Monitor to adjust its position.

10. Move the CTI to end of the clip and again drag on the oval in the Monitor to create a final keyframed position.

11. Move through the clip and make more Position adjustments, adding keyframes automatically, so that the oval stays on your subject.

Click on the **Show Keyframe Controls** button (the stopwatch) in the upper right of the panel to open the **Applied Effects** panel timeline, as illustrated above.

9   Set an initial keyframe

Move the **CTI** playhead to the beginning of the clip.

Click the **Toggle Animation** button (the stopwatch to the right of the **Motion** listing) to begin a keyframing session.

A set of little diamond-shaped keyframe points will be added at the position of the **CTI** for each of the **Motion** property's settings.

If the position of the white oval needs to be adjusted in your video frame, click on the oval in the **Monitor** panel and move it so that it is over the person you want to highlight.

10   Set an ending keyframe

Move the **CTI** to the end of your video clip.

Again click on the white oval in the **Monitor** panel and drag it so that it again covers the person you want to highlight.

If necessary, you can also adjust the **Scale** settings so that the oval is larger or smaller, as needed.

Diamond-shaped keyframe points will automatically be added at the position of the **CTI** for any adjustments you've made to the **Position** or **Scale** settings.

Highlight a Person in a Crowd (Part 3)

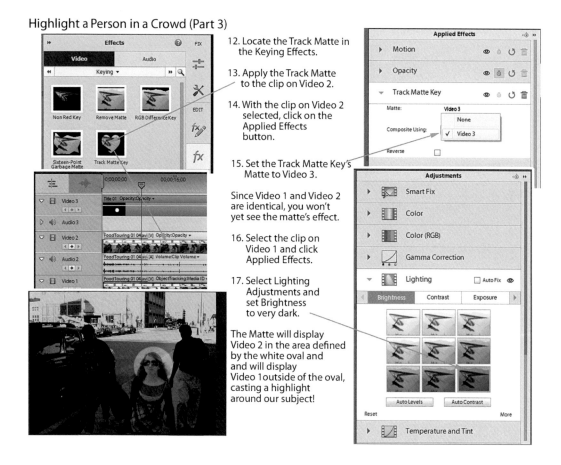

12. Locate the Track Matte in the Keying Effects.

13. Apply the Track Matte to the clip on Video 2.

14. With the clip on Video 2 selected, click on the Applied Effects button.

15. Set the Track Matte Key's Matte to Video 3.

Since Video 1 and Video 2 are identical, you won't yet see the matte's effect.

16. Select the clip on Video 1 and click Applied Effects.

17. Select Lighting Adjustments and set Brightness to very dark.

The Matte will display Video 2 in the area defined by the white oval and and will display Video 1 outside of the oval, casting a highlight around our subject!

11 Add other keyframes as needed

"Scrub" through your clip (by dragging the **CTI** back and forth) to ensure that the white oval covers the person you want to highlight throughout the clip.

As necessary, click on the white oval on the **Monitor** and drag it into **Position** over the person you're highlighting.

New keyframes will automatically be added at the **CTI's** position whenever you make an adjustment.

Using these keyframes, Premiere Elements will create the necessary animation to follow the person you want to highlight around the video frame throughout your video clip.

12 Locate the Track Matte effect

Click the **Effects** button on the program's **Toolbar**.

The **Track Matte** is located in the **Keying** category of **Video Effects**.

13 **Apply the Track Matte to the Video 2 clip**

Drag the **Track Matte** effect onto the clip on the Video 2 track.

14 **Open the Applied Effects panel for the Video 2 clip**

Click to select the Video 2 clip and then click the **Applied Effects** button on the right side of the interface.

The clip's **Applied Effects** panel will open.

15 **Set the Track Matte to Video 3**

Click on the **Track Matte** listing to open its settings and properties.

From the effect's **Matte** drop-down menu, select Video 3, as illustrated on the facing page.

In other words, the **Track Matte** is being applied to the clip on Video 2, but we are telling it to define the matte's shape and position using the white oval graphic we placed on Video 3.

You've just created a tracking object and used it to define a matte!

The area defined by the white oval in your video frame is displaying the video on Video 2. Everything outside of that oval is displaying the video on Video 1.

However, since at this point both clips are identical, you won't yet be able to see the results of this effect. But that will change in a moment – when we apply an effect to one or the other clip.

16 **Open the Adjustments panel for Video 1**

Click to select on the clip on Video 1 and then click the **Adjustments** button at the top of the program's **Toolbar**.

The **Adjustments** panel will open.

17 **Adjust the Brightness for Video 1**

Click on the **Lighting** listing on the **Adjustments** panel.

Select a dark setting (the lower right button) from the **Quick Fix** grid or click the **More** button and darken the clip using the slider.

The area in your video frame defined by the oval should remain bright (displaying the clip on Video 2) while everything outside of the oval's position will be dimmed (displaying the darkened clip on Video 1).

Also, because we keyframed motion so that the white oval will follow the person around the video frame, our subject will remain highlighted throughout the clip no matter where in the video frame he or she moves!

COOL TRICK

30 Blur a Face as on "COPS"

You've got a classic post-production problem.

You've shot some terrific footage – but one of the people in your video doesn't *want* to be in your video! Or maybe you don't have a signed release to legally show his or her face. Or maybe there's just something objectionable in your shot (e.g., nudity) that you don't want to impose on your audience.

As anyone who's familiar with reality TV shows like "COPS" knows, the *spot blur* – blurring specific spots or rendering specific areas in your video indistinguishable – is often the easiest way to censor a face or object.

Creating a spot blur using the **Track Matte** is very similar to *Cool Trick 29, Highlighting a Person in a Crowd*. In fact, we'll reuse many of the same steps.

The difference is that, instead of darkening the clip on Video 1 so that everything *outside* the matte is affected, we'll apply a **Mosaic** effect to the clip on Video 2 so that everything *inside* the matte area is blurred.

1   **Place your clip on Video 1**

   Drag your clip from the **Project Assets** panel to the Video 1 track on your timeline.

2   **Place the same clip on Video 2**

   Drag the same clip from the **Project Assets** panel to the Video 2 track, directly above the first clip.

   These two clips should be identical and aligned, one above the other, as in the illustration.

3   **Open the Title Adjustments workspace**

   We will create our tracking object by drawing the shape in Premiere Elements **Title Adjustments** workspace. You could, as an alternative, create your shape, using a program like Photoshop Elements, save it as a PSD with no background layer and import into your Premiere Elements project.

   To create a shape in the **Title Adjustments** workspace, position the **CTI** to the very beginning of your clips and select **New Text/ Default Text** from the program's **Text** menu.

   The **Title Adjustments** panel will open and the placeholder words "Add Text" will appear on the **Monitor** panel.

Blur a Face as on "COPS" (Part 1)

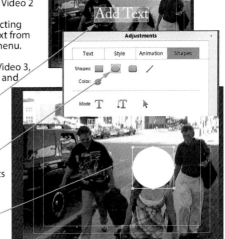

1. Add your clip to Video 1

2. Add identical clip to Video 2

3. Create a title by selecting New Text/Default Text from the program's Text menu.

Ensure your title is on Video 3, above your other clips, and is stretched to the same length.

4. Delete the placeholder text.

5. Select the Oval shape tool from the Title Adjustments Shapes tools.

6. Draw an oval over the person you want to highlight.

You may need to stop at this point and ensure that your title is in position, directly above your clips, and that it is stretched on the timeline, if necessary, so that it is the same duration as your video clips, as illustrated on the previous page. To re-open the **Title Adjustments** panel, double-click on the title.

4   Delete the placeholder text

When the **Default Text** title opens, select this placeholder text and press the **Delete** key on your keyboard to remove it.

5   Select the Oval shape tool

Click to select the **Shapes** tab in the **Title Adjustments** panel and select the oval shape.

6   Draw an oval over the area you want to highlight

Drag the **Oval** shape tool to create a white oval over the person you want to highlight in your video. (To constrain this shape to a circle, hold down the **Shift** key as you drag.)

Once you've drawn the oval, you can switch to the **Selection Tool** (the arrow) and tweak its size and position.

Click on the timeline to exit the **Title Adjustments** workspace. Your timeline should now show your video clip on Video 1 and Video 2 and your graphic on Video 3.

For **Step 7** through **Step 15**, we'll use exactly the same process we used to keyframe the motion of our tracking object in *Cool Trick 29, Highlighting a Person in a Crowd*.

Blur a Face as on "COPS" (Part 2)

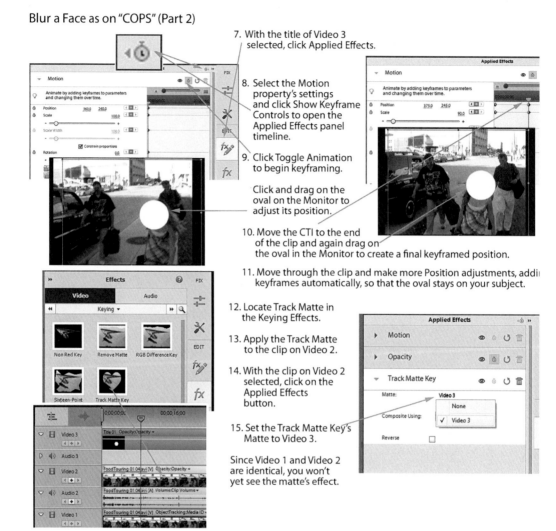

7. With the title of Video 3 selected, click Applied Effects.

8. Select the Motion property's settings and click Show Keyframe Controls to open the Applied Effects panel timeline.

9. Click Toggle Animation to begin keyframing.

Click and drag on the oval on the Monitor to adjust its position.

10. Move the CTI to the end of the clip and again drag on the oval in the Monitor to create a final keyframed position.

11. Move through the clip and make more Position adjustments, adding keyframes automatically, so that the oval stays on your subject.

12. Locate Track Matte in the Keying Effects.

13. Apply the Track Matte to the clip on Video 2.

14. With the clip on Video 2 selected, click on the Applied Effects button.

15. Set the Track Matte Key's Matte to Video 3.

Since Video 1 and Video 2 are identical at this point, you won't yet see the matte's effect.

As in *Cool Trick 29*, since both clips are identical at this point, you won't yet be able to see the results of this effect. But that will change in a moment – when we apply an effect to one of the clips.

16   Locate the Mosaic effect

Click the **Effects** button on the program's **Toolbar.**

The **Mosaic** effect is located in the **Stylize** category of **Video Effects.**

The **Mosaic** effect produces a pixelated distortion of your image.

As an alternative, you can use the **Gaussian Blur** effect, located in the **Blur & Sharpen** category of **Video Effects.**

Blur a Face as on "COPS" (Part 3)

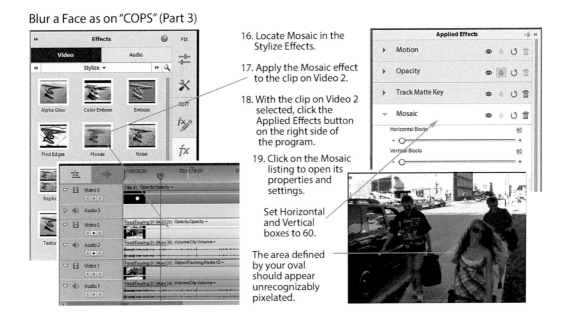

16. Locate Mosaic in the Stylize Effects.

17. Apply the Mosaic effect to the clip on Video 2.

18. With the clip on Video 2 selected, click the Applied Effects button on the right side of the program.

19. Click on the Mosaic listing to open its properties and settings.

Set Horizontal and Vertical boxes to 60.

The area defined by your oval should appear unrecognizably pixelated.

17 Apply the Mosaic effect to Video 2

Drag the effect onto the clip on the Video 2 track.

18 Open the Applied Effects panel for Video 2

Click to select the Video 2 clip and then click the **Applied Effects** button on the right side of the interface.

The clip's **Applied Effects** panel will open.

19 Adjust the Mosaic effect for Video 2

Click on the **Mosaic** listing in the **Applied Effects** panel to display the effect's properties and settings.

Using the sliders or by typing in the numbers, set the **Horizontal Blocks** and **Vertical Blocks** both to about 60 (or whatever your particular situation requires).

As you adjust the **Mosaic** settings, the person you've tracked with your white oval should become unrecognizably pixelated.

Track Matte effects can be a bit temperamental, by the way. So, if you need to change the keyframed motion track for the white oval or swap in a different blur or distortion effect, you may need to completely remove the **Track Matte** from the clip and re-apply it.

31 Add Soft Edges to a Dream Sequence

Most often, you'll use the **Track Matte** to create a moving matte, a transparent area that follows, or *tracks*, an object or person around your video frame (hence the name **Track Matte**).

But, because the **Track Matte** also creates semi-opaque masks (based on the shape and colors you're using to define your matte), you can also use it to create a stationary video effect.

One such effect is the soft, feathered edge – a blurring of the edges of your video frame commonly used to give the impression of a dream sequence.

To create this effect, you'll need a white graphic with a black gradient edge, like the one in the illustration. You can download my free DreamSequence.jpg from the Products page of Muvipix.com.

Import it into your Premiere Elements project by browsing to it using **Add Media** and then selecting **PC Files and Folders**.

1 Place a video clip on Video 1

Drag the video clip you'd like to use for your dream sequence from the **Project Assets** panel to the Video 1 track on your timeline.

2 Place the same clip on Video 2

Drag the same clip from the **Project Assets** panel to the Video 2 track, directly above the first clip.

These two clips should be identical and aligned, one above the other.

3 Place DreamSequence.jpg on Video 3

Drag the graphic DreamSequence.jpg from the **Project Assets** panel to Video 3, directly above your other video clips.

It should fill your video frame, covering the clips on Video 1 and Video 2 completely. If not, click on it in the **Monitor** panel and, by dragging the corner handles that appear, scale and position it as needed.

You may need to stop at this point and ensure that your Dreamsequence graphic is in position, directly above your clips, and that it is stretched, if necessary, to the same duration as your video clips, as illustrated on the facing page.

Add Soft Edges to a Dream Sequence

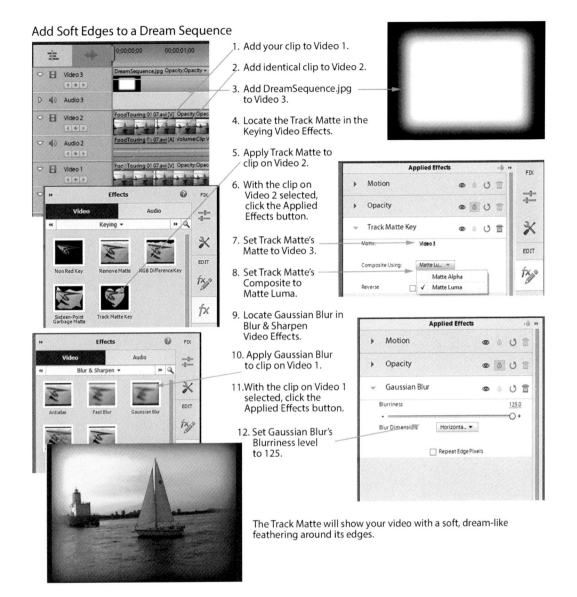

1. Add your clip to Video 1.

2. Add identical clip to Video 2.

3. Add DreamSequence.jpg to Video 3.

4. Locate the Track Matte in the Keying Video Effects.

5. Apply Track Matte to clip on Video 2.

6. With the clip on Video 2 selected, click the Applied Effects button.

7. Set Track Matte's Matte to Video 3.

8. Set Track Matte's Composite to Matte Luma.

9. Locate Gaussian Blur in Blur & Sharpen Video Effects.

10. Apply Gaussian Blur to clip on Video 1.

11. With the clip on Video 1 selected, click the Applied Effects button.

12. Set Gaussian Blur's Blurriness level to 125.

The Track Matte will show your video with a soft, dream-like feathering around its edges.

---

4 **Locate the Track Matte effect**

Click the **Effects** button on the program's **Toolbar**.

The **Track Matte** is located in the **Keying** category of **Video Effects**.

5 **Apply the Track Matte to the Video 2 clip**

Drag the **Track Matte** effect onto the clip on the Video 2 track.

6 **Open the Applied Effects panel for the Video 2 clip**

Click to select the Video 2 clip and then click the **Applied Effects** button on the right side of the interface.

The clip's **Applied Effects** panel will open.

7   Set the Track Matte to Video 3

Click on the **Track Matte** listing on the **Applied Effects** panel to open its properties and settings.

From the effect's **Matte** drop-down menu, select **Video 3**.

8   Set the Track Matte Composite to Matte Luma

From the **Track Matte's Composite** drop-down menu, select the **Matte Luma** option.

At this point, although the **Track Matte** is creating a mask based on DreamSequence.jpg, you won't see any real effect, since the clip on Video 1 and the clip on Video 2 are identical.

However, once we apply a blur to the clip on Video 1, the effect of the mask will become much more obvious.

9   Locate the Gaussian Blur effect

Click the **Effects** button on the program's **Toolbar**.

The **Gaussian Blur** effect is located in the **Blur & Sharpen** category of effects.

10   Apply the Gaussian Blur effect to Video 1

Drag the effect onto the clip on the Video 1 track.

HOT TIP
Matte Alpha vs. Matte Luma Mattes

In the **Applied Effects** panel settings for the **Track Matte**, you may notice that the **Composite Setting** can be toggled to either **Matte Alpha** or **Matte Luma**.

Matte Alpha, the default setting, bases the location of its matte on the white object with no background on a track above it (i.e., the white oval we use in *Cool Trick 29* and *Cool Trick 30*).

Matte Luma, on the other hand (which we use in *Cool Trick 31*), uses a white *and black* pattern or shape on an upper track not only to determine the *position* of its matte but also the levels of its *opacity*, or transparency. In other words, if you have your **Track Matte** set to **Matte Luma**, the whiter the shape or shapes on your tracking clip, the more opaque the matte will appear. The blacker the shape or background on the tracking image, the more transparent the matte. When using **Matte Luma**, for instance, you may well use a white shape on a black background to define your matte area rather than a white shape with no background.

11   Open the Applied Effects panel for Video 1

Click to select the Video 1 clip and then click the **Applied Effects** button on the right side of the interface.

The clip's **Applied Effects** panel will open.

12   Adjust the Gaussian Blur effect for Video 1

Click on the **Gaussian Blur** listing in the **Applied Effects** panel to open its properties and settings.

Using the sliders or by typing in the numbers, set the **Blurriness** level to about 125.

Your video should appear in the **Monitor** with a soft, blurry edge – a classic dream sequence!

Chapter 10
Cool Picture-in-Picture Tricks
Doubling up your videos

There are lots of cool things you can do with more than one video on screen at once.

Even more if you animate their sizes and positions in your video frame.

A **Picture-in-Picture** is a video inset within another video.

In other words, a **Picture-in-Picture** (commonly called "**PiP**") is made up of a larger video – usually full screen – with a smaller video floating over it, usually in one corner of the video frame.

A **PiP** can be used to show two video sources at the same time. (Many TVs are equipped with a **PiP** system so that a viewer can monitor two channels at the same time.) A **PiP** can also have a thematic purpose. It can be used, for instance, to tell a story by showing the subject being discussed as the main video and the person telling the story as an inset in one corner of the screen.

But **PiPs** need not be stationary. The inset video can be animated so that it moves around the video frame and even changes size. And, as we demonstrate in *Cool Trick 33*, the main video and the inset can even be animated to swap places!

And, as we demonstrate in *Cool Trick 34*, you can also use a **PiP** as a special effect – positioning the inset video so that it appears to be showing on a TV in the main video!

COOL TRICK

32 Make a Basic Picture-in-Picture

Virtually all **Picture-in-Picture** effects are set up the same basic way: A master video is placed on the Video 1 track and a second video – **Scaled** and **Positioned** as necessary – is placed on the Video 2 track, directly above it.

Beyond that, there are no rules for a **Picture-in-Picture**. The two video sources can be sized and positioned to interact with each other in any number of ways. And, with a little keyframing, you can even animate how each transitions on and off screen!

1 **Place main video on Video 1**

Drag your main video from the **Project Assets** panel to the Video 1 track.

2 **Place your PiP video on Video 2**

Drag the video you will use as your **PiP** from the **Project Assets** panel to the Video 2 track, positioned directly above the main video, as in the illustration on the next page.

When in this position, your **PiP** video will fill your video frame, so you will not be able to see your main video in your **Monitor** panel.

Make a Basic Picture-in-Picture

1. Add your main video to Video 1.

2. Add your PiP video to Video 2.

3. Click to select PiP video in Monitor.

   Corner handles will appear around video.

4. Drag in corner handles to change PiP's Scale.

5. Drag PiP into Position in Monitor panel.

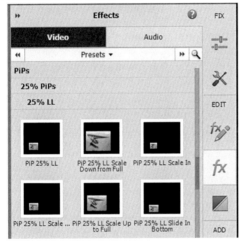

The PiP category of Preset effects includes nearly 200 Picture-in-Picture effects, most of which are animated and all of which are applied by simply dragging the preset onto the Video 2 clip.

Presets that include the words "in" or "out" in their names are animated and will transition your PiP in or out and can be combined on the same clip.

3   Select the PiP in your Monitor

Click on the **PiP** video in your **Monitor** panel.

A frame with corner handles will appear around your video.

4   Drag corner handles to resize your PiP

Drag one of the corner handles on the selected video inwards in the **Monitor** panel.

As you do, the video clip will resize.

5   Drag your PiP into position

Once you've resized your **PiP** video clip, click on it and drag it into position within your video frame.

And that's really all there is to creating a basic **Picture-in-Picture**!

Once you've created your **Picture-in-Picture**, you can do a number of things to make it more interesting. Using keyframing, you can set it to change its position and/or size over the course of the clip.

You can also use keyframing to make your **PiP** appear by zooming in from 0% **Scale** and/or disappear by zooming out to 0% *Scale*. (For more information on creating motion keyframes for your **Picture-in-Picture** effect, see *Cool Trick 34, Use a PiP as a Transition*.)

You can also use a **Preset Video Effect** to automatically create your **PiP**, once you've placed video clips on Video 1 and Video 2.

The **PiP** presets can be found by clicking the **Effects** button on the program's **Toolbar** and then selecting the **Presets** category from **Video Effects**. The program comes with nearly 200 **Picture-in-Picture** presets.

Nearly 175 of these **Presets** include keyframed motion. And so, by simply dragging a preset onto a clip on Video 2, you can not only create instant **PiPs**, but you can add a variety of eye-catching animations to it too!

COOL TRICK

33 Swap Your Inset and Main Video in a PiP

This one is kind of fun. Sort of a **Picture-in-Picture** juggling act.

In this *Cool Trick*, we'll create a **Picture-in-Picture** – but then we'll swap the main video with the inset image so that the main video becomes the inset image and vice versa.

1   **Place Clip 1 on Video 1**

     Drag Clip 1, the video you will use initially as your main video, from the **Project Assets** panel to the Video 1 track.

2   **Place Clip 2 on Video 2**

     Drag Clip 2, the video you will use as your initial **PiP**, from the **Project Assets** panel to the Video 2 track, positioned directly above the main video, as in the illustration on the next page.

     When in this position, Clip 2 will, at first, fill your video frame, so you will not be able to see your main video in your **Monitor** panel.

3   **Open Clips 2's Applied Effects panel**

     Click to select the Video 2 clip and then click the **Applied Effects** button on the right side of the interface.

     The clip's **Applied Effects** panel will open.

Swap Your Inset and Main Video in a PiP (Part 1)

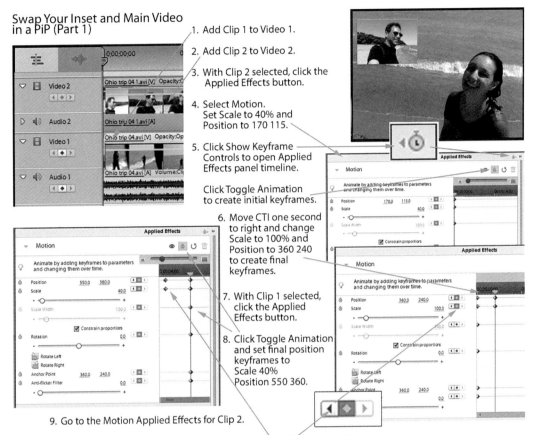

1. Add Clip 1 to Video 1.

2. Add Clip 2 to Video 2.

3. With Clip 2 selected, click the Applied Effects button.

4. Select Motion.
   Set Scale to 40% and Position to 170 115.

5. Click Show Keyframe Controls to open Applied Effects panel timeline.

   Click Toggle Animation to create initial keyframes.

6. Move CTI one second to right and change Scale to 100% and Position to 360 240 to create final keyframes.

7. With Clip 1 selected, click the Applied Effects button.

8. Click Toggle Animation and set final position keyframes to Scale 40% Position 550 360.

9. Go to the Motion Applied Effects for Clip 2.

10. Click Previous Keyframe button for Motion to jump CTI to first keyframe set.

11. Go to the Motion Applied Effects for Clip 1.

12. With CTI synced to Clip 2's first keyframe position, set Scale to 100% and Position to 360 240.

4 Set Clips 2's Scale and Position

Click the **Motion** listing on the Applied Effects panel to open its properties and settings.

Set **Scale** to 40%.
Set **Position** to 145 115. (For high-def, use 465 285.)

Clip 2 should now appear as a **Picture-in-Picture** inset in the upper left of your video frame, overlaying Clip 1.

5 Set Clip 2's initial keyframe

Click the **Show Keyframe Controls** button (the stopwatch) in the upper right of the **Applied Effects** panel to open the **Applied Effects** panel timeline, as in the illustration above.

Move your **CTI** playhead to the point at which you'd like your **PiP** swap to begin.

Click the **Toggle Animation** button (the stopwatch) to the right of the **Motion** property's listing.

A set of keyframe points will appear at the position of the **CTI** on the **Applied Effects** panel timeline.

6 Set the final Clip 2 keyframe

Move the **CTI** about a second to the right on the **Applied Effects** panel timeline and change the **Motion** property's settings, either by using the slider or overwriting the numbers:

> Set **Scale** 100%.
> Set **Position** 360 240. (For high-def, use 960 540.)

(If you are using the PAL standard definition video, set this keyframe's **Position** to 360 288.)

As you change these settings, a new set of keyframe points will automatically be created at the **CTI's** position for **Scale** and **Position**.

At this point, Clip 2 should fill your video frame.

You have now created keyframed animation in which Clip 2 will go from an inset in the upper left corner of your video frame to a full screen video.

We'll now create the *reverse* of this keyframed animation for Clip 1. In order to synchronize the motion paths for these two clips, make sure you leave the **CTI** at its position over the keyframe set we created in **Step 6**.

Note that, because Clip 2 is covering the entire video frame at this point, we will not be able to see the effect of changing these settings in the next few steps.

7 Open Clips 1's Applied Effects panel

Click to select the Video 1 clip on your timeline and then click the **Applied Effects** button on the right side of the interface.

The clip's **Applied Effects** panel will open.

8 Set the final Clip 1 keyframe

Since the **CTI** is already at the position of Clip 2's final keyframe, we'll first set Clip 1's final keyframe and then later go back and set its initial keyframe.

Click the **Motion** listing on the **Applied Effects** panel to open its properties and settings.

If the **Applied Effects** panel timeline is not visible, click the **Show Keyframe Controls** button, as you did in **Step 5**.

Click the **Toggle Animation** button (the stopwatch) to the right of the **Motion** property's listing.

A set of keyframe points will appear at the position of the **CTI** on the **Applied Effects** panel timeline.

> Set **Scale** to 35%.
> Set **Position** to 575 375. (For high-def, use 1455 795.)

This will position Clip 1 in the lower right of the video frame (although you won't yet be able to see this because Clip 2 is covering up the entire video frame at this point).

In order to ensure that our initial keyframe for Clip 1 is in exactly the same place in your video as the initial keyframe for Clip 2, we'll jump between the **Applied Effects** panels for each clip.

9   Open Clips 2's Applied Effects panel

In many cases, you can simply click to select Clip 2 on your timeline and the Clip 2 **Applied Effects** panel will display. If the **Applied Effects** panel timeline closes when you select Clip 2 on your timeline, however, you will need to re-open it.

Click the **Show Keyframe Controls** button to re-open the **Applied Effects** panel timeline.

10   Jump to Clip 2's initial keyframes

Click the **Previous Keyframe** button for either **Position** or **Scale**, as illustrated on page 125.

The **CTI** will jump to Clip 2's initial keyframes.

11   Open Clips 1's Applied Effects panel

Click to select Clip 1 on your timeline. If the **Applied Effects** panel timeline closes when you select Clip 2 on your timeline, you will need to re-open it.

Again click the **Show Keyframe Controls** button to re-open the **Applied Effects** panel timeline.

12   Set the initial Clip 1 keyframe

Leaving the **CTI** at its current position, change the **Motion** properties settings either by using the slider or overwriting the numbers:

> Set **Scale** to 100%.
> Set **Position** to 360 240. (For high-def, use 960 540.)

Swap Your Inset and Main Video in a PiP (Part 2)

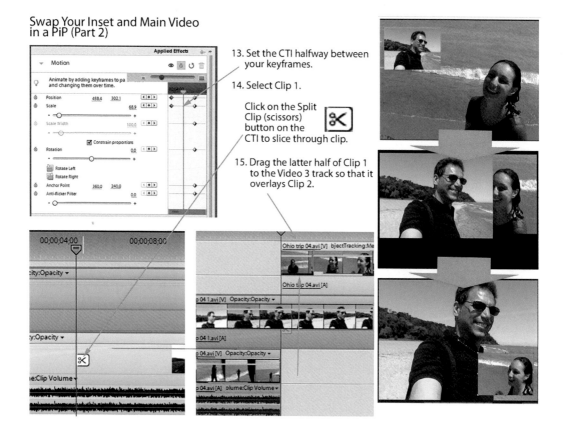

13. Set the CTI halfway between your keyframes.

14. Select Clip 1.

Click on the Split Clip (scissors) button on the CTI to slice through clip.

15. Drag the latter half of Clip 1 to the Video 3 track so that it overlays Clip 2.

If you are using the PAL video system, set this keyframe's **Position** to 360 288.

As you change these settings, a new set of keyframe points will automatically be created at the **CTI's** position for **Scale** and **Position**.

We've now created all of the keyframes necessary for our swap – but, unfortunately, we have a small problem. When Clip 2 scales to 100% it covers up our Clip 1's **Picture-in-Picture**!

So, in order for this effect to work, we'll have to somehow get Clip 1 on a video track *above* Clip 2 as the two clips swapping **Scale** and **Position** settings.

To do this, we'll split Clip 1 halfway through its transition from main video to inset and then we'll drag the latter half of this clip up to Video 3. We should be able to do this without our viewers being too aware of the move.

13 Set the CTI halfway through the Motion path

Position the **CTI** playhead on the **Applied Effects** panel timeline about halfway between the keyframe points we've created for Clip 1, as illustrated above.

14 Split Clip 1

Clip 1 should be selected on your timeline. If not, click on it so that it is selected.

Click the **Split Clip** (scissors icon) button on the **CTI** playhead.

Clip 1 will be sliced through at the position of the CTI.

15 Drag the latter half of Clip 1 to Video 3

Click and drag the latter segment of Clip 1 up to Video 3, directly above its current position. (You can use the **CTI**, at its current position, to help you line up the clip's position.)

If your timeline does not yet have a Video 3 track, drag the clip up above Video 2 anyway.

When you release your mouse button, the Video 3 track will automatically be created and your clip will appear on it.

When you play your video, you should see the **Picture-in-Picture** swap out – the inset becoming the main video and the main video becoming the inset.

There will be a slight jump as Clip 1 suddenly moves above Clip 2 about midway through the motion. But it should seem to be a natural part of the transition from one **PiP** arrangement to the other.

COOL TRICK

34 Use a PiP as a Transition

When you combine keyframing with a **Picture-in-Picture**, you can create all sorts of animations and motion. (In fact, as we discuss after *Cool Trick 32*, Premiere Elements includes nearly 175 animated **PiP Preset Effects**.)

And, by combining a **Picture-in-Picture** effect with custom keyframed animation, you can create your own unique transition!

In order to create this transitional effect, you'll need for the outgoing clip (Clip 1) to be on an upper video track (Video 2, in this example) and the next clip (Clip 2) to be on a track below it (Video 1, in this example) overlapped by Clip 1 by about one second, as illustrated on the next page.

Use a PiP as a Transition

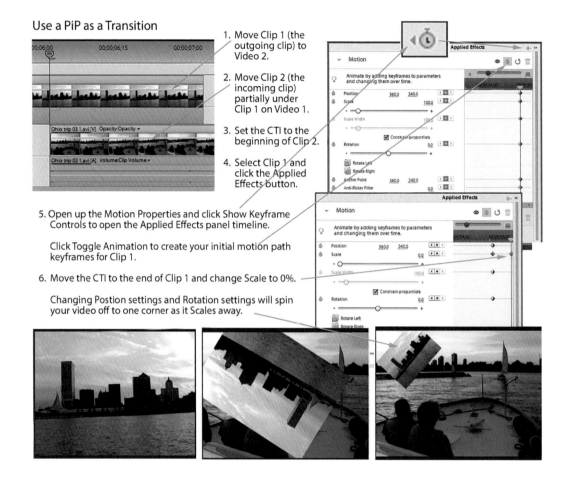

1. Move Clip 1 (the outgoing clip) to Video 2.

2. Move Clip 2 (the incoming clip) partially under Clip 1 on Video 1.

3. Set the CTI to the beginning of Clip 2.

4. Select Clip 1 and click the Applied Effects button.

5. Open up the Motion Properties and click Show Keyframe Controls to open the Applied Effects panel timeline.

   Click Toggle Animation to create your initial motion path keyframes for Clip 1.

6. Move the CTI to the end of Clip 1 and change Scale to 0%.

   Changing Postion settings and Rotation settings will spin your video off to one corner as it Scales away.

1 Place Clip 1 on Video 2

Drag Clip 1 from the **Project Assets** panel to the Video 2 track. Or, if you've already got a timeline built, slide Clip 1 from the Video 1 track up to Video 2.

2 Place Clip 2 partially under Clip 1

Drag Clip 2 to the Video 1 track so that it is partially overlapped by Clip 1 on the timeline. This overlapped segment should be at least one second, as illustrated above.

3 Move the CTI to the beginning of Clip 2

You can do this by either manually dragging the CTI playhead or by selecting Clip 2 (on the Video 1 track) and pressing the **Page Up** key on your keyboard.

4   Open Clip 1's Applied Effects panel

Click to select Clip 1 (on the Video 2 track) and then click the **Applied Effects** button on the right side of the interface.

The clip's **Applied Effects** panel will open.

5   Create Clip 1's initial Motion keyframes

Click on the **Motion** listing in the **Applied Effects** panel to open its properties and settings.

Click the **Show Keyframe Controls** button (the stopwatch) on the upper right of the panel to open the **Applied Effects** panel timeline, as in the illustration.

Click the **Toggle Animation** button (the stopwatch) to the right of the **Motion** listing. A set of keyframe points will be created for the **Motion** properties at the position of the **CTI**.

6   Create Clip 1's final Motion keyframes

Move the **CTI** to just before the end of Clip 1 on the **Applied effects** panel timeline.

Set **Scale** to 0%.

When you play the timeline, Clip 1 will shrink and then disappear in the center of your video frame, revealing Clip 2 in its place.

And that's fine for a basic transition.

But you can also have some fun here and add whatever else you'd like to make this transitional animation interesting.

If you set the **Position** for this final keyframe to 40 25, the clip will zoom off to the upper left corner as it shrinks away.

If you set the **Position** for this final keyframe to 680 25, the clip will zoom off to the upper right.

A **Position** keyframe setting of 40 455 sends it to the lower left.
A **Position** keyframe setting of 680 455 sends it to the lower right.

And, if you change the final **Rotation** numbers, you can make the clip spin as it disappears off into space!

By typing **Rotation** numbers that are greater than 360 degrees, you can set up the animation so that your clip spins several times on its way out.

Type in 990 degrees as your final keyframe for **Rotation.** This sets the keyframed effect to 2x270 – so the clip will now spin away through two and three-quarters rotations on the way off-screen!

Make Your Video Look Like It's on TV

1. Add your TV background clip (Clip 1) to Video 1.

2. Add your TV image (Clip 2) to Video 2.

3. Click on Clip 2 in your Monitor. Corner handles will appear around the clip.

4. Drag the corner handles inward to reduce the clip's Scale.

5. Drag the clip into position so that it appears to be on the TV.

If there is camera movement in your background clip, use keyframing to keep Clip 2 in position on the TV screen.

COOL TRICK

35 Make Your Video Look Like It's on TV

You may not think of this special effect as a **Picture-in-Picture** trick, but it's set up essentially the same way. You have a main video (your scene background) and your have an inset image (the video that you'll position so that it looks like it's on TV).

Naturally, you can also use this same effect to make your video look like it's showing on a big movie screen and even to make it look like it's being projected on the side of a building!

1 Place your background video on Video 1

Drag your main video (Clip 1) – the TV background clip – from the **Project Assets** panel to the Video 1 track.

2 Place your inset video on Video 2

Drag the video you want to use as your TV video (Clip 2) from the **Project Assets** panel onto the Video 2 track, directly above your background clip.

At this point, because it is on an upper track and not yet **Scaled**, Clip 2 will fill your video frame and you will not be able to see Clip 1.

3   **Select Clip 2 in your Monitor**

Click on the **Clip 2** in the **Monitor** panel.

A frame with corner handles will appear around your video, as in the illustration.

4   **Drag corner handles to resize Clip 2**

Drag one of the corner handles on the selected video inwards on the **Monitor** panel.

As you do, the video clip will resize.

5   **Drag Clip 2 into position**

Once you've resized your **PiP** video clip, click on it and drag it into position so that it appears to be on the TV in Clip 1. You can also rotate it a bit as necessary by hovering your mouse over a corner handle until the double-headed arrow appears and then dragging.

More precise **Scale, Position** and **Rotation** settings can be made by opening the **Applied Effects** panel for the clip.

If your shot of the TV is from an angle rather than straight on, you can add some perspective to your inset shot by applying the **Basic 3D** effect (from the **Perspective** category of effects) to your video and adjusting its **Swivel** and **Tilt**.

And that's pretty much all there is to it! Your video will look it's on TV!

If you really want to bring this special effect to the next level, you can use a background video that includes some camera motion – say a pan from the TV to a reaction shot of someone watching the TV. You'll then use keyframing to synchronize the **Position** and **Scale** of Clip 2 so that it remains in position on the TV even as the TV itself moves within your video frame.

Chapter 11

Cool "Key" Tricks

Magic effects with transparency

Chroma Key and Videomerge are two of the most powerful (and fun) video effects in the Premiere Elements toolkit.

Using these effects, you can make someone appear to be in almost any location on Earth – or even beyond!

You can also make him or her appear to do superhuman things – like fly!

Other Key tricks allow you to mix video sources so that you can make a person appear to confront his own twin!

Whether you're aware of it or not, you've encountered **Chroma Key** (and its variations in **Green Screen** and **Blue Screen**) countless times.

Every time you watch a televised weather report – the weather person apparently standing in front of satellite video and moving maps – you're actually seeing a **Chroma Key** effect. That weather person is, in reality, standing in front of a plain green screen, electronics removing this green background and replacing it with the weather graphics for the broadcast.

Virtually every movie that includes scenes of live humans interacting with special effects is using some form of **Chroma Key** – as the actors, like the weather person, perform in front of a green or blue background which is later swapped with some new background or effect.

What's most amazing about these special effects is that essentially the very same technology that allows big Hollywood movie studios to swap out backgrounds, make people appear to be hundreds of feet tall and even make super-heroes appear to fly is available on your home computer with Premiere Elements.

The method of using the effect is fairly simple. And once you understand how it works (and maybe how to combine it with keyframed motion), you'll be able to create many of these same big-screen Hollywood effects at home.

Here's how it works, basically: You shoot your subject standing in front of an evenly-colored screen – usually bright green or blue (colors that are not present in human skin tones). This clip is placed on an upper video track.

A new background is placed on a lower video track, directly below it.

A **Key** effect is applied to the clip on the upper track and its "key" color is set to the color of the background. **Chroma Key** or **Videomerge** then

HOT TIP
The Mac version doesn't include Chroma Key

As we've indicated elsewhere in this book, the Mac version of Premiere Elements 2018 omits a few effects and transitions that are included in the PC version. Perhaps the greatest omissions of the set, however, are Key effects – **Chroma Key, Green Screen Key** and **Blue Screen Key** – vital tools in any post-production toolkit.

Fortunately, the Mac version does include **Videomerge** (described in the sidebar on page 139), a simplified version of the **Chroma Key** effect that, in most cases, can be substituted for it.

We use the **Videomerge** effect in place of the **Chroma Key** effect in *Cool Trick 37* and, on a Mac, it can be used similarly in place of **Chroma Key** to any of this chapter's effects.

makes that green or blue "key-colored" background transparent – making it appear that your subject is standing in front of whatever video you've placed on the video track below it!

Throughout the *Cool Tricks* in this chapter, I'll refer rather generically to the **Chroma Key** effect. However, you may find that the **Green Screen Key**, **Blue Screen Key** or even **Videomerge** will work more effectively for your particular needs or situation.

Don't be afraid to experiment and see which **Keying** effect works best for you!

COOL TRICK

36 Make a Person Look Like He's Someplace Else

This is the simplest and most basic **Chroma Key** effect.

We'll take a person shot in front of a green screen – and we'll make him look like he is someplace exotic, like at the foot of the Great Pyramid.

But just because it's a basic effect doesn't mean it isn't a great one! Basic as it is, this is the special effect used in virtually all of Hollywood's big-budget science fiction and fantasy films!

HOT TIP
A successful Chroma Key depends on a well-shot scene

No matter which of the **Key** effects you use – **Chroma Key, Green Screen Key, Blue Screen Key** or even **Videomerge** – the success of your effect depends very much on how well shot your "key," or foreground, video is.

Two things are vitally important:

- The background you use for this video, whether green, blue or whatever, should be of a flat, even color and it should be as evenly lit as possible. You want to avoid hot spots or shadows. Remember, the program will make this area transparent based on the color range you set. And the narrower that range – the more even the color of the background – the smoother your "key" and the less the likelihood that you'll have to widen your color range so much that your "key" will leak into the areas you don't want to make transparent.

- Your foreground (the actor or other objects you don't want removed by the **Chroma Key** effect) should also be well lit. And, of course, don't include the color you're going to "key" in the costume or props that this actor will be using or it will become transparent too!

Make a Person Look Like He's Someplace Else

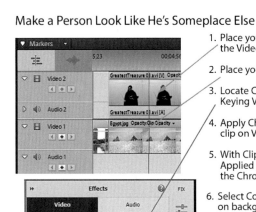

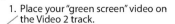

1. Place your "green screen" video on the Video 2 track.

2. Place your background on Video 1.

3. Locate Chroma Key in the Keying Video Effects.

4. Apply Chroma Key to the clip on Video 2.

5. With Clip 2 selected, click Applied Effects and open the Chroma Key settings.

6. Select Color eyedropper and click on background to sample it.

7. Adjust Similarity and Blend, then Threshold, Cutoff and Smoothing to remove background.

Working temporarily in Mask Only mode allows you to focus on removing the background while leaving your subject intact.

1 Place your "key" video on Video 2

Drag your "key" video (Clip 2) – the video of your subject in front of a green or blue screen – from the **Project Assets** panel to the Video 2 track.

2 Place your background video on Video 1

Drag the video or still you want to swap in as your new background (Clip 1) from the **Project Assets** panel to the Video 1 track. Trim or extend it as necessary so that it has the same duration as your Key clip.

3 Locate the Chroma Key effect

Click the **Effects** button on the program's **Toolbar**.

Chroma Key is located in the **Keying** category of **Video Effects**.

4 Apply Chroma Key to the Video 2 clip

Click to select Clip 2 (on Video 2) and drag the **Chroma Key** effect onto it.

You may or may not see an immediate effect. In most cases, you should see some transparency in your clip, although it may not yet be "keyed" to your background color. (**Chroma Key** is, in fact, keyed by default to sort of a mid-gray.)

5 Open Clip 2's Applied Effects panel

With Clip 2 selected on your timeline, click the **Applied Effects** button on the right side of the program.

Clip 2's **Applied Effects** panel will open.

6 Set the "key" color

Click on the **Chroma Key** listing on the **Applied Effects** panel to open the effect's properties and settings.

Click on the eyedropper next to the color swatch at the **Color** property listing, as illustrated on the facing page. Your mouse cursor will turn into an eyedropper.

Click on the green background on Clip 2 in your **Monitor**. Try to find a nice representative sample of the color's mid-range.

Your **Color** swatch should change to the color of the area you sampled and much of your clip's background should become transparent, revealing Clip 1 through it

---

HOT TIP
Videomerge

Videomerge is Adobe's simplified version of the **Chroma Key** effect. It functions essentially the same way – removing an evenly-colored background and making it transparent so that you can replace it with an alternative background. Its controls, however, are much simpler – consisting pretty much of a tolerance level slider for setting the color range for the background to be keyed. In many cases, it can work at least as effectively as or even better than **Chroma Key**! (We put it to use in *Cool Trick 37.*)

Videomerge can be added to a clip a number of ways, including dragging it from the **Videomerge** category on the **Video Effects** panel and by **right-clicking** on a clip and selecting **Apply Videomerge** from the **Clip** sub-menu.

The program will even offer to run **Videomerge** automatically, by default, whenever you add a clip with an even-colored background to your timeline. To disable this sometimes annoying feature, go to the **General** page on the program's **Preferences** (under the **Edit** menu on a PC). Uncheck the box next to **Show All Do Not Show Again Messages**.

7 **Adjust your Key**

Adjusting your **Chroma Key** properties so that they remove the green background and yet leave your subject intact is about finding a balance, for the most part, between **Similarity** (which widens the range of color that will be keyed) and **Blend** (which controls how transparent the elements in your clip are).

If your "key" clip is well shot, there should be enough distinction between your subject and the background that adjusting **Similarity** alone removes virtually all of the background.

Threshold, Cutoff and **Smoothing** are fine tuning adjustments. You're best not adjusting them until you've done all you can with **Similarity** and **Blend**.

The *Hot Tip* below discusses some of the program's more advanced tools for producing and fine tuning your key effect.

HOT TIP
Tweaking your "key"

One very effective way to fine tune your **Chroma Key** is to check the **Mask Only** option in the **Chroma Key** properties. This will show you a white silhouette of your keyed image so that you can focus on removing the keyed area while maintaining the integrity of your subject, as in the illustration on the previous page.

Once you've completed your **Similarity** and **Blend** adjustments in **Mask Only** mode, uncheck the box to return to regular view and adjust the other properties as needed.

If there are areas of your background you can't seem to remove – either because they were lit unevenly or because the edge of your green screen shows, for instance – you may be able to manually remove them by using one of the **Garbage Mattes**. (In fact, that's why they're called **Garbage Mattes**. They're for removing unwanted "trash" from your video.)

To most effectively set up a **Garbage Matte**, apply it either before you apply your **Chroma Key,** or temporarily disable your **Chroma Key** effect (by clicking on the little black eyeball to the right of the effect's listing in the **Applied Effects** panel). This will allow you to see exactly what you're cutting off with this **Matte**.

As we show you in *Cool Trick 38*, the area of a **Garbage Matte** is defined by the placement of four, eight or sixteen corner points. And, as with the **Crop** effect, by dragging these corner handles into position, you define the opaque area. The area outside of this **Garbage Matte** area is cropped off or rendered transparent.

Once you've set up your **Garbage Matte**, you can re-enable your **Chroma Key** effect by clicking again on the eyeball to the right of the effect's listing.

37 Make a Person Appear to Fly

This *Cool Trick* has a lot in common with *Cool Trick 36*. Again we'll be shooting our subject in front of a green screen. And again we'll be keying out the background so that we can replace it with a new background.

In this exercise, we'll use **Videomerge** to create the special effect. But you can also use **Chroma Key** if you prefer (or if it gives you better results), applying and customizing it as described in *Cool Trick 36*, *Cool Trick 39* or *Cool Trick 40*.

This time out we'll be adding a new element to our effect: *Motion*. In addition to using the **Videomerge** effect to swap in a new background, we'll be using some **Motion** keyframing to animate our subject so that he doesn't just appear within our new background – he'll seem to shoot across the sky!

For this effect to work, it's as important to have a strong background clip as it is to have a well-shot foreground. In my case, I used some video I shot of an F-16 fly-by at a recent air show – so not only do I have video of the sky but, in the foreground of this clip, I've got a crowd of people looking up in awe!

As I created my keyframed motion path for my actor, I matched his position in the sky with the position of the jet in my background video. That way it looked like the crowd was watching my actor fly overhead.

Your background video doesn't need to be quite so full of motion, however. You'll just as likely wow your audience by simply having your actor appear to fly over a city skyline or over your neighborhood's rooftops.

1   Place your "key" video on Video 2

Drag your "key" video (Clip 2) – the video of your subject in front of a green screen – from the **Project Assets** panel to the Video 2 track.

In my demo, I'm using video I made of an actor standing in front of a green screen, his arms extended above him.

I could just as easily have had him lie on his belly across some chairs draped with my green screen material. But, when he is standing, his hair and cape are hanging back behind him. Once I rotate his clip 90 degrees, it will appear that they are being blown back by the wind as he flies.

For added effect, I could have also had a fan blowing on him so that his hair and cape appear to flutter as he "flies" through the scene.

2   Place your background video on Video 1

Drag the video or still you want to use as your background (Clip 1) from the **Project Assets** panel to the Video 1 track, directly below Clip 2.

Make a Person Appear to Fly

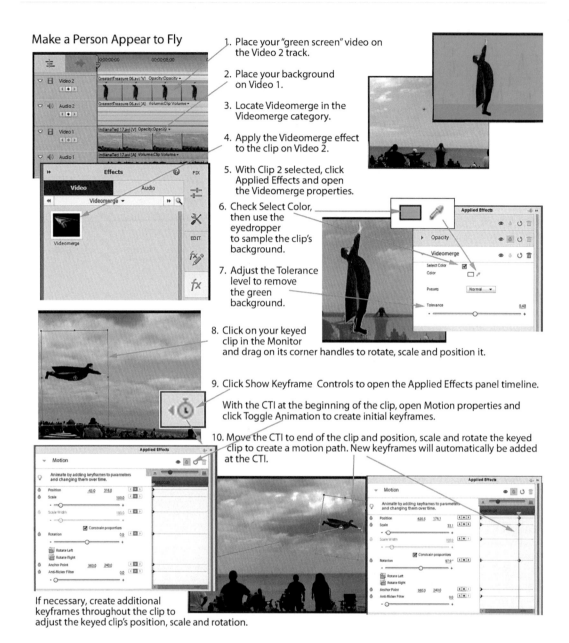

1. Place your "green screen" video on the Video 2 track.

2. Place your background on Video 1.

3. Locate Videomerge in the Videomerge category.

4. Apply the Videomerge effect to the clip on Video 2.

5. With Clip 2 selected, click Applied Effects and open the Videomerge properties.

6. Check Select Color, then use the eyedropper to sample the clip's background.

7. Adjust the Tolerance level to remove the green background.

8. Click on your keyed clip in the Monitor and drag on its corner handles to rotate, scale and position it.

9. Click Show Keyframe Controls to open the Applied Effects panel timeline.

   With the CTI at the beginning of the clip, open Motion properties and click Toggle Animation to create initial keyframes.

10. Move the CTI to end of the clip and position, scale and rotate the keyed clip to create a motion path. New keyframes will automatically be added at the CTI.

If necessary, create additional keyframes throughout the clip to adjust the keyed clip's position, scale and rotation.

3 Locate the Videomerge effect

Click the **Effects** button on the program's **Toolbar**.

Videomerge is located in the **Videomerge** category of **Video Effects**.

4 Apply Videomerge to Clip 2

Drag the **Videomerge** effect onto Clip 2.

You can also apply **Videomerge** by **right-clicking** on the clip on your timeline and then selecting **Apply Videomerge** from the **Clip** sub-menu.

In most cases, you should see some transparency in your clip as soon as the effect is applied – although it may not yet be completely "keyed."

5   Open Clip 2's Applied Effects panel

Select Clip 2 on your timeline and click the **Applied Effects** button on the right side of the program.

Clip 2's **Applied Effects** panel will open.

6   Set the "key" color

Click on the **Videomerge** listing on the **Applied Effects** panel to open the effect's properties and settings.

Check the option to **Select Color** at the top of these settings. This will make the color sampler (eyedropper), next to the color swatch in the **Color** properties, available.

Click on this eyedropper. Your mouse cursor will turn into an eyedropper.

Click on the green background behind your actor in the **Monitor** panel.

Your **Color** swatch should change to green (or your background color) and most of the green background should become transparent, revealing Clip 1 through it.

7   Adjust your Key

Adjust the **Videomerge** effect's **Tolerance** level. **Tolerance** sets how wide a range of color is "keyed." The higher the level you set, the wider the variation from your key color will be keyed.

If, with **Tolerance** set all the way to 1.00, you still aren't able to key out the entire background of your clip, this means that your foreground clip's background does not have an even enough color range to create a successful **Videomerge** or **Chroma Key** effect.

You may be able to remove some of the more challenging spots around the outside of your video frame using one of the **Garbage Mattes** we describe in *Cool Trick 38*.

But, as we discussed in the *Hot Tip* on page 137, if your green screen is not an even enough range of color, with no hot spots or shadows, you will not be able to create an effective **Videomerge** or **Chroma Key** effect.

Once our actor's background has been completely removed, we'll adjust his **Rotation**, **Scale** and **Position** (settings of the **Motion** property) so that he appears to be a part of our background video clip.

8 Scale, Position and Rotate Clip 2

Press the **Page Up** key on your keyboard to make sure your **CTI** playhead is at the beginning of your clip (or the point at which your flying actor will make his appearance in the scene).

Click on the clip of the actor in your **Monitor** panel. You should see a frame with four corners appear around the edge of the video, as in the illustration on page 142. (If not, ensure that the **Motion** property is selected in the **Applied Effects** panel before you click on the clip.)

Drag in on the corner handles to **Scale** the actor to any size.

If you hover your mouse just outside of this clip's corner handles, a double-headed arrow will appear. When it does, click and drag to adjust the **Rotation** of the clip.

HOT TIP
Keying Effects

Keying effects are effects which make portions of your video clip transparent. Each has its strengths, and one may be more effective in a given situation than another. Two or more can also be used together on the same clip. It's very common, for instance to use a **Garbage Matte** to trim away as much of a background as possible before applying **Chroma Key**.

Chroma Key is an all-purpose keying effect which can be set to make any color in your clip transparent. The **Blue Screen Key** and the **Green Screen Key** function similarly but are preset to the blue and green hues that are most commonly used as backgrounds for keyed clips. The **RGB Difference Matte** also works similarly to **Chroma Key**. However, it is most effective on clips which include bright color and few shadows.

The **Non Red Key** is most effective for removing greens and blues from a clip, and is often added to a clip which already has a Key effect applied in order to fine tune the effect and reduce edge fringing. Likewise, the **Remove Matte** is often applied to a clip that has been Keyed in order to fine tune the effect and tweak halos around the edge of the key.

The **Luma Key** will create transparency in a clip by making its brightest areas transparent, based on the level of brightness that you set.

The **Difference Matte Key** is used as a means of keying out shared imagery from two clips, one placed above the other on your timeline.

Alpha Adjust is used (often in conjunction with other Keying effects) to adjust the opacity of the transparent area.

Garbage Mattes create masks, or transparent areas, in a variety shapes that are determined by the positions of their four, eight or sixteen corner points.

The **Image Matte Key** and the **Track Matte Key** create transparency in your video clip based on the location of the graphic on a video track above it. We do some interesting things with the **Track Matte Key** in **Chapter 9, Cool Track Matte Tricks**.

Click and drag on the actor to adjust his **Position** in the video frame.

Drag your actor to his "starting position" in your scene. If you'd like your actor to appear to fly in from the left side of your frame, for instance, drag him as far off the left side of the frame as you can.

9   **Set an initial keyframe for the Video 2 clip**

Click on the **Motion** listing in the **Applied Effects** panel to open the **Motion** properties and settings. If necessary, manually type in **Position** settings to move your actor off-screen.

Click the **Show Keyframe Controls** button (the stopwatch) on the upper right of the panel to open the **Applied Effects** panel timeline, as in the illustration on page 142.

Click **Toggle Animation** (the stopwatch icon) to the right of the **Motion** listing. A set of keyframe points will appear at the position of the **CTI**.

10   **Set a final keyframe for the Video 2 clip**

Move the **CTI** to the end your video clip (or the point at which your actor will fly off-screen).

Again click on your actor in the **Monitor** panel and drag him to his final position in the frame (or, if he's to fly out of the frame, as far off the edge of the frame as you can). You can also adjust his **Rotation** and **Scale** if you'd like, either by dragging on his clip's corner handles or by adjusting the numbers or sliders in the **Applied Effects** panel.

As you do, new keyframes will be added at the **CTI's** position.

Premiere Elements will create the motion path animation of your actor flying between these two sets of keyframes.

Scrub through (by dragging the **CTI**) or play your video to see how the animation looks. (You may need to press the **Enter** key to **Render** your video first in order to preview it at full quality.)

If you'd like, you can add more keyframes so that your actor changes directions or rotates as he flies by.

And, if you drag him into a new position using an arc rather than in a direct line, Premiere Elements will even create a *curved* rather than straight motion path between the keyframes!

Of course, for maximum effect, you'll want to add a classic Superman "whoosh" sound effect to your audio track for the scene and maybe a stirring John Williams-like musical score!

Have a Person Confront His Twin

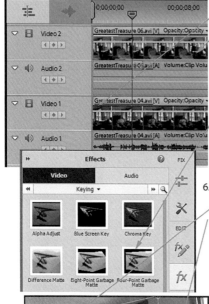

1. Place Clip 1 on the Video 1 track.

2. Place Clip 2 on Video 2.

3. Locate one of the Garbage Mattes in the Key category of Video Effects.

4. Apply the Garbage Matte to the clip on Video 2.

5. With Clip 2 selected, click the Applied Effects button to open the Applied Effects panel.

6. Click to select the Garbage Matte listing in the Applied Effects panel and shape matte by dragging corner handles in the Monitor panel.

COOL TRICK

38 Have a Person Confront His Twin

Here's a fun Key *Cool Trick* that's also surprisingly simple!

For this *Cool Trick*, we'll take two shots of an actor in the same scene and then composite them together. The result: Our actor will find himself looking eye-to-eye with his exact double!

This effect can, of course, also be accomplished using **Chroma Key**. You could shoot your actor in front of a green screen and then composite that clip with another clip of him or her in a scene. (Similarly to our basic **Chroma Key** *Cool Trick 36*.) For this version of this *Cool Trick*, however, we'll use another of the **Keying** effects – the **Garbage Matte**.

By taking two identical shots of an actor in the same scene (one of which positions him on the left side of the scene and the other of which positions him on the right), we'll create a composite by masking areas of one shot and replacing these masked areas with areas from the other shot.

The challenge is, of course, to get two shots that match up perfectly. You'll definitely want to shoot both videos with your camcorder locked down on a tripod.

And, if you're using natural lighting, you'll want to shoot both clips within a few of minutes of each other so that there are minimal differences in the sunlight, etc.

If possible, you may even want to lock down your camcorder's automatic white balance so that it doesn't shift your color tones trying to compensate for a changed costume or another environmental issue. And certainly be aware of drapes, cushions or other props or background objects that may have changed positions between shots.

1 Place Clip 1 on Video 1

Drag Clip 1 of your actor from the **Project Assets** panel to the Video 1 track.

2 Place Clip 2 on Video 2

Drag Clip 2 of your actor from the **Project Assets** panel to the Video 2 track, directly above Clip 1.

3 Locate the Garbage Matte effect

Click the **Effects** button on the program's **Toolbar**.

The **Garbage Matte** effects are located in the **Keying** category of **Video Effects**.

There are three **Garbage Matte** effects – a four-point, an eight-point and a sixteen-point. They all function the same way: You define an area in your video, the shape of which you "draw" by positioning the corner points, and everything outside of that area will be cropped away or, more accurately, masked or made transparent, revealing the clip(s) on the video track(s) below.

Which **Garbage Matte** you use depends on how complicated the area is that you want to matte. I usually start with a simple **Four-Point Garbage Matte** and, if it's not precise enough, I delete it and try the **Eight-Point Garbage Matte** and so on. (If the area you want to define is perfectly rectangular, you could even use the **Crop** effect instead if you'd like!)

The Garbage Matte masks, or makes transparent, the video outside of the matte area you define.

4   **Apply the Garbage Matte to Clip 2**

Click to select Clip 2 on Video 2 and drag the **Garbage Matte** effect onto it.

The default shape of your **Garbage Matte** will mask part of your Clip 2, revealing Clip 1 clip below it.

5   **Open Clip 2's Applied Effects panel**

With Clip 2 selected, click on the **Applied Effects** button on the right side of the program.

Clip 2's **Applied Effects** panel will open.

6   **Adjust the Garbage Matte's position**

Click on the **Garbage Matte's** listing in the **Applied Effects** panel to open the effect's properties and settings.

The **Applied Effects** panel will list each of the points that define the shape of your **Garbage Matte** (the area of Clip 2 that will be visible) and their locations. The numbers following the names of each points are vector positions, measured in pixels from the upper left corner of the video frame. The first number is the horizontal distance from the upper left corner and the second is the vertical measurement.

Although you can set the locations of each of these points by manually changing these vector numbers, you can more intuitively change their locations and the shape of your matte by simply dragging them around right on the **Monitor** panel!

Ensure the **Garbage Matte's** listing is selected on the **Applied Effects** panel. The **Garbage Matte's** area will appear in your **Monitor** panel, the corner handles appearing as crosshairs inside circles around the matte.

To change the positions of these points, just click and drag on them.

If your two clips are well matched (and your actor didn't cross over the imaginary line separating them in the two shots), it should be pretty easy to shape your **Garbage Matte** so that both shots of your actor are displayed – apparently sharing the same scene!

If your actor moves through the scene and you need to follow him or her with the **Garbage Matte**, you can keyframe the positions of the **Garbage Matte** points so that the matte changes position and shape as necessary over the course of the clip.

And, of course, if you're really ambitious, you can have the same actor appear a *third* time by adding another layer of matted video!

COOL TRICK

39 Make Someone Look Very Small (or Huge)

Although many special effects shots can be created by simply combining a single green screen clip and background with a **Keying** effect, you're by no means limited to a single keyed clip for a given sequence.

For this *Cool Trick*, we'll use two layers of keyed clips over a single background – making it appear that our actress (who will appear to be a mere 10 inches tall) is being pursued by an enormous giant.

To accomplish this effect, then, we'll need three clips:

- **Clip 1** – A background clip with enough recognizable props or furnishings that your viewers will be able to tell that your actors are disproportionately sized. In my example, I'm using a shot of my living room, captured from floor level.

- **Clip 2** – Our actor, shot in front of a green screen. For maximum effect, he or she should match the lighting and camera angle of the background clip as much as possible. In my case, I've shot my actress looking up and reacting to an attack by an imaginary monster. I also shot her fleeing off screen so that my scene would have movement.

- **Clip 3** – The giant, also shot in front of a green screen. For my shot, I again set the camera up at floor level and shot my actor just from his knees down. You could also use a dog, cat, parakeet or even a toy or a hand puppet for your monster. In my example, my giant will seem to step into the scene.

When my clips are combined and composited, it will appear that the giant walks into the scene and the miniature actress screams and runs off-screen.

1 **Place your background video on Video 1**

Drag Clip 1 (the background) from the **Project Assets** panel to the Video 1 track.

2 **Place Clip 2 on Video 2**

Drag Clip 2 (the actress) from the **Project Assets** panel to the Video 2 track.

3 **Locate the Chroma Key effect**

Click the **Effects** button on the program's **Toolbar**.

Chroma Key is located in the **Keying** category of **Video Effects**. (Naturally, you can use the **Videomerge** effect, located in the **Videomerge** category of effects, instead.)

Make a Person Look Very Small (or Huge)

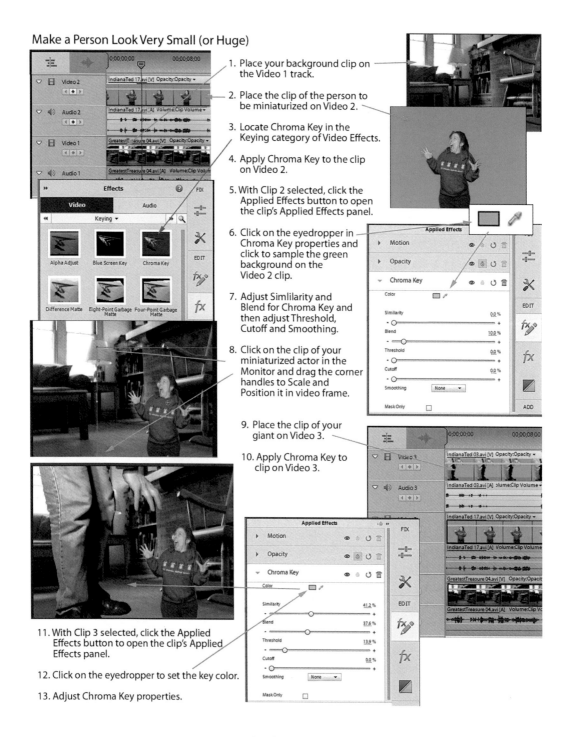

1. Place your background clip on the Video 1 track.

2. Place the clip of the person to be miniaturized on Video 2.

3. Locate Chroma Key in the Keying category of Video Effects.

4. Apply Chroma Key to the clip on Video 2.

5. With Clip 2 selected, click the Applied Effects button to open the clip's Applied Effects panel.

6. Click on the eyedropper in Chroma Key properties and click to sample the green background on the Video 2 clip.

7. Adjust Simlilarity and Blend for Chroma Key and then adjust Threshold, Cutoff and Smoothing.

8. Click on the clip of your miniaturized actor in the Monitor and drag the corner handles to Scale and Position it in video frame.

9. Place the clip of your giant on Video 3.

10. Apply Chroma Key to clip on Video 3.

11. With Clip 3 selected, click the Applied Effects button to open the clip's Applied Effects panel.

12. Click on the eyedropper to set the key color.

13. Adjust Chroma Key properties.

4   Apply Chroma Key to Clip 2

Click to select Clip 2 on Video 2 and drag the **Chroma Key** effect onto it.

You may or may not see an immediate effect. In most cases, you should see some transparency in your clip, although it may not yet be "keyed" to your background color. (**Chroma Key** is, in fact, keyed by default to the color white.)

5 **Open Clip 2's Applied Effects panel**

With Clip 2 selected on your timeline, click the **Applied Effects** button on the right side of the program.

Clip 2's **Applied Effects** panel will open.

6 **Set the "key" color**

Click on the **Chroma Key** listing in the **Applied Effects** panel to open the effect's properties and settings.

Click on the eyedropper next to the color swatch at the **Color** property listing. Your mouse cursor will turn into an eyedropper.

Click on Clip 2's green background on the **Monitor** panel. Try to find a nice representative sample of the color's mid-range.

7 **Adjust your Key**

Adjust your **Chroma Key Similarity** and **Blend** sliders so that they remove the green background and yet leave your subject intact.

Threshold, Cutoff and **Smoothing** are fine tuning adjustments. You're best not adjusting them until you've done all you can with **Similarity** and **Blend**.

(For hints on tweaking your "key," see my *Hot Tip* on page 144.)

Now that the actress's background has been removed, we'll adjust her **Scale** and **Position** (settings of the **Motion** property) so that she appears to be very small within our background video clip.

8 **Scale and Position the Video 2 clip**

Click on the clip of the actor or actress in your **Monitor** panel. You should see a frame with four corner handles appear around the edge of the video, as in the illustration on the previous page.

Drag in on the corner handles to **Scale** the actor to any size.

Click and drag on the actor to adjust his or her **Position** in the video frame.

We'll now add another layer of effects to the scene – our enormous giant. The process is essentially the same: we'll add the clip to an upper video track and then make the green background transparent.

9   **Place Clip 3 to Video 3**

Drag Clip 3 (the giant) from the **Project Assets** panel to the Video 3 track.

10   **Apply Chroma Key to Clip 3**

Click the **Effects** button on the program's **Toolbar**.

Drag the **Chroma Key** effect onto Clip 3.

11   **Open Video 3's Applied Effects panel**

With Video 3 selected, click the **Applied Effects** button on the right side of the program.

The **Applied Effects** panel for the Video 3 clip will open.

12   **Set the "key" color**

As you did with Clip 2 in **Step 6**, click on the **Chroma Key** listing in the **Applied Effects** panel to open the effect's properties and settings and set up your key.

13   **Adjust your Key**

As you did in **Step 7**, adjust the **Chroma Key** settings for Clip 3 so that they remove the green background.

If necessary, you can adjust Clip 3's **Scale** and **Position** to exaggerate your monster's size – and enrich the whole scene with sound effects and music!

COOL TRICK

40 Add a Blast or Explosion to a Scene

Although green and blue are the most common colors "keyed" in a video (because they are colors not found in human skin tones), they're by no means the only colors you can make transparent with **Chroma Key** or **Videomerge**.

Any flat, consistent color can be "keyed" in a clip – even black. Sometimes the results aren't quite as neat and clean as the results you get when working with green or blue screen. But, particularly in a quick sequence or an effect shot (such as an explosion), the effect often goes by so quickly that your audience may not even notice if the edges aren't quite perfect.

We've got some free clips of blasts and explosions over black backgrounds at Muvipix.com. You can also find lots of great free and affordable explosion footage at www.detonationfilms.com.

Add a Blast or Explosion to a Scene

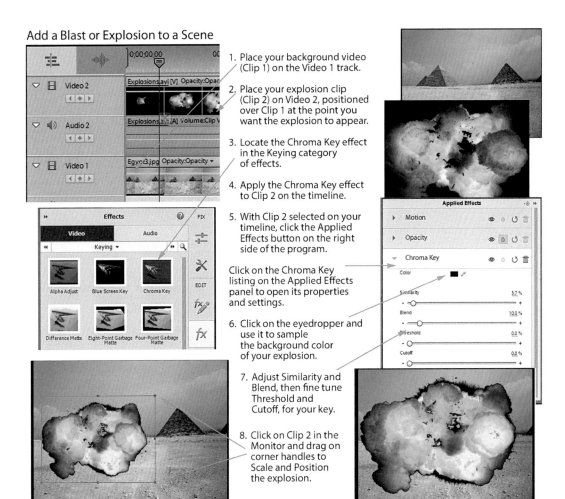

1. Place your background video (Clip 1) on the Video 1 track.

2. Place your explosion clip (Clip 2) on Video 2, positioned over Clip 1 at the point you want the explosion to appear.

3. Locate the Chroma Key effect in the Keying category of effects.

4. Apply the Chroma Key effect to Clip 2 on the timeline.

5. With Clip 2 selected on your timeline, click the Applied Effects button on the right side of the program.

   Click on the Chroma Key listing on the Applied Effects panel to open its properties and settings.

6. Click on the eyedropper and use it to sample the background color of your explosion.

7. Adjust Similarity and Blend, then fine tune Threshold and Cutoff, for your key.

8. Click on Clip 2 in the Monitor and drag on corner handles to Scale and Position the explosion.

---

1   Place your background video on Video 1

Drag Clip 1, your background, from the **Project Assets** panel to the Video 1 track.

2   Place your explosion clip on Video 2

Drag your footage of an explosion (Clip 2) from the **Project Assets** panel to the Video 2 track, positioned over the segment of Clip 1, beginning at the point at which you'd like your explosion to appear.

3   Locate the Chroma Key effect

Click the **Effects** button on the program's **Toolbar**.

Chroma Key is located in the **Keying** category of **Video Effects**.

4   Apply Chroma Key to the Video 2 clip

Click to select Clip 2 (the Key clip) on Video 2 and drag the **Chroma Key** effect onto it.

You may or may not see an immediate effect. In most cases, you should see some transparency in your clip, although it may not yet be "keyed" to your background color. (**Chroma Key** is, in fact, keyed by default to a mid-gray.)

5   Open Clip 2's Applied Effects panel

Select Clip 2 on your timeline and click the **Applied Effects** button on the right side of the program.

The **Applied Effects** panel for Clip 2 will open.

6   Set the "key" color

Click on the **Chroma Key** listing in the **Applied Effects** panel to open the effect's properties and settings.

Click on the eyedropper next to the color swatch at the **Color** property listing. Your mouse cursor will turn into an eyedropper.

Click on area of Clip 2's black background. Try to find a nice representative sample of the background color.

Your **Color** swatch should change to the color of the area you sampled and much of your clip's background should become transparent, revealing Clip 1 clip through it.

7   Adjust your Key

Adjust your **Chroma Key Similarity** and **Blend** sliders so that they remove the green background and yet leave your subject intact.

Threshold, Cutoff and **Smoothing** are fine tuning adjustments. You're best not adjusting them until you've done all you can with **Similarity** and **Blend**.

(For hints on tweaking your "key", see my *Hot Tip* on page 144.)

8   Scale and Position the explosion

Click on the clip of the explosion on your **Monitor** panel. A frame will appear around the clip as well as four corner handles.

Drag the corner handles in to **Scale** the clip smaller. Click and drag on the clip to **Position** it in your video frame.

Naturally, you can have several explosions in your scene, layered on top of one another, if you'd like. You can even **Chroma Key** in an actor so that he appears to be in front of the explosion – or even between two layers of explosions!

COOL TRICK
41 Create an Explosion in the Sky

In many ways, this *Cool Trick* is the opposite of *Cool Trick 40*. Rather than using a **Keying** effect to make the area around an explosion transparent so that we can make it appear over a background scene, we'll make an area of the *scenery* transparent so that the explosion seems to be *behind* it!

This *Cool Trick* works best if your background video has got a nice, clear sky – and none of your foreground imagery includes any color similar to the sky's. In other words, we'll essentially be using the sky as our "blue screen," then using the **Chroma Key** (or **Videomerge**) effect to make the blue areas transparent.

If your sky doesn't remove as cleanly as you'd like, you can, of course, supplement your **Chroma Key** or **Videomerge** with one of the **Garbage Mattes** – manually cropping away the stubborn or difficult areas. Or, if the background or skyline in your clip is relatively square, you can even use one of the **Garbage Mattes** all by itself to create the effect. (For more information on using the **Garbage Mattes** to make areas in your video transparent, see *Cool Trick 38, Have a Person Confront His Twin*.)

And, of course, you aren't limited to using this effect to create an explosion in the sky. You can also replace your blue sky with, say, a giant or monster that seems to be standing over the skyline or rooftops – or you can replace the clear, blue sky in your scene with dark storm clouds or even an approaching tornado!

To create the effect, you'll need two clips:

- **A clip of an explosion.** You'll find some free stock footage of explosions on Muvipix.com and a wide variety of free and low-cost explosion clips at www.detonationfilms.com.

- **A scene of a skyline** of some type. It can be a row of houses or a city skyline, and you can use a video clip or a still image. (I'll be using a photograph of the Pyramids.) The most important thing is that either the sky be a smooth color blue (so that it can be **Chroma Keyed** out) or the line between your foreground imagery and the sky behind it be straight and even enough that you can shape a **Garbage Matte** around it.

    1 **Place your skyline video on Video 1**

    Drag the video or still of your skyline (Clip 1) from the **Project Assets** panel to the Video 1 track.

Create an Explosion in the Sky

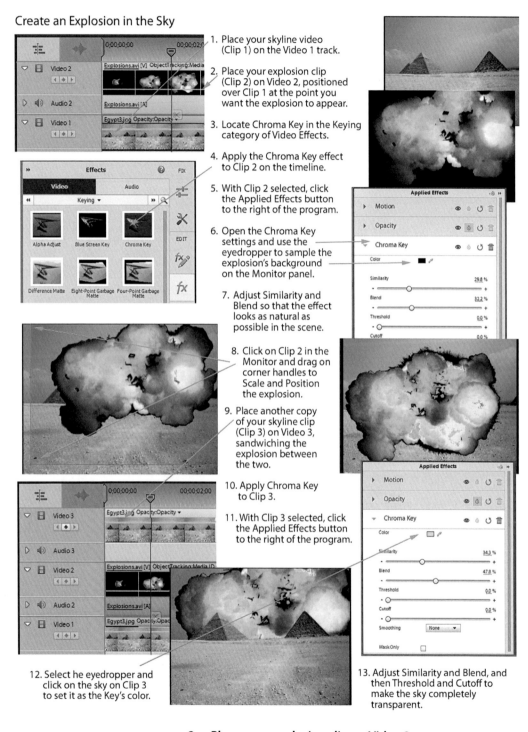

1. Place your skyline video (Clip 1) on the Video 1 track.

2. Place your explosion clip (Clip 2) on Video 2, positioned over Clip 1 at the point you want the explosion to appear.

3. Locate Chroma Key in the Keying category of Video Effects.

4. Apply the Chroma Key effect to Clip 2 on the timeline.

5. With Clip 2 selected, click the Applied Effects button to the right of the program.

6. Open the Chroma Key settings and use the eyedropper to sample the explosion's background on the Monitor panel.

7. Adjust Similarity and Blend so that the effect looks as natural as possible in the scene.

8. Click on Clip 2 in the Monitor and drag on corner handles to Scale and Position the explosion.

9. Place another copy of your skyline clip (Clip 3) on Video 3, sandwiching the explosion between the two.

10. Apply Chroma Key to Clip 3.

11. With Clip 3 selected, click the Applied Effects button to the right of the program.

12. Select he eyedropper and click on the sky on Clip 3 to set it as the Key's color.

13. Adjust Similarity and Blend, and then Threshold and Cutoff to make the sky completely transparent.

2   **Place your explosion clip on Video 2**

Drag the footage of your explosion (Clip 2) from the **Project Assets** panel to the Video 2 track.

Position your explosion clip on your timeline at the point at which you'd like the explosion to occur.

Because we'll want sky in the background up to the point that our explosion occurs, we'll sandwich the explosion (on the Video 2 track) in between two copies of our skyline clip (one on the Video 1 track, the other on the Video 3 track).

After we apply the **Chroma Key** effect to the clip on the Video 3 track, the sky from the clip on Video 1 will show through this transparent area, giving us what will appear to be our original skyline clip – until the explosion appears.

3   **Locate the Chroma Key effect**

Click the **Effects** button on the program's **Toolbar**.

Chroma Key is located in the **Keying** category of effects.

4   **Apply Chroma Key to the Video 2 clip**

Drag the **Chroma Key** effect onto Clip 2 (the explosion).

You may or may not see an immediate effect. In most cases, you should see some transparency in your clip, although it may not yet be "keyed" to your background color. (**Chroma Key** is, in fact, keyed by default to a mid-gray.)

5   **Open Clip 2's Applied Effects panel**

Select Clip 2 on your timeline and click the **Applied Effects** button on the right side of the program.

The **Applied Effects** panel for Clip 2 will open.

6   **Set the "key" color**

Click on the **Chroma Key** listing in the **Applied Effects** panel to open the effect's properties and settings.

Click on the eyedropper next to the color swatch at the **Color** property listing. Your mouse cursor will turn into an eyedropper.

Click on an area of Clip 2's black background. Try to find a nice representative sample of this background color.

Your **Color** swatch should change to the color of the area you sampled and much of your clip's background should become transparent, revealing Clip 1 clip through it.

7   **Adjust your Key**

Adjust your **Chroma Key** properties sliders so that they remove the background and yet leave the explosion intact.

(For hints on tweaking **your "key,"** see my *Hot Tip* on page 144.)

8   Scale and Position the explosion

Click on the clip of the explosion on your **Monitor** panel. A frame will appear around the clip as well as four corner handles.

Drag the corner handles in or out to **Scale** the clip smaller. Click and drag on the clip to **Position** it in your video frame.

Now that we have the explosion in position, we'll overlay both clips with another copy of our scenery/skyline clip and then use **Chroma Key** (or the **Garbage Matte**, if you prefer) to remove the sky from it.

9   Place a copy of the skyline clip on Video 3

Drag the video or still of your skyline (Clip 3) from the **Project Assets** panel to the Video 3 track. You'll want to position it directly over the skyline clip on the Video 1 track so that both clips line up perfectly.

Until we add the **Chroma Key** effect to it, the clip we've added to Video 3 will be the only one we'll see in the **Monitor** panel.

10   Apply Chroma Key to Clip 3

Drag the **Chroma Key** effect onto Clip 3 (the skyline).

11   Open Video 3's Applied Effects panel

With the clip on Video 3 selected, click the **Applied Effects** button on the right side of the program.

The **Applied Effects** panel for the Video 3 clip will open.

12   Set the "key" color

As you did with Clip 2 in **Step 6**, click on the **Chroma Key** listing in the **Applied Effects** panel to open the effect's properties and settings to set up your key and set the "key" color. In this case, though, your "key" color will be the sky above the scenery.

13   Adjust your Key

As you did in **Step 7**, adjust the **Chroma Key** settings for Clip 3 so that they remove the sky.

If you manually drag (or "scrub") your **CTI** playhead through the scene or play the video, it should begin with what appears to be your skyline scene (though it's actually Clip 3, with its sky transparent, and Clip 1 appearing through it).

And then suddenly that sky behind the skyline (the Pyramids, in my example) will erupt into a huge explosion!

Chapter 12

Cool Motion Tracking Tricks

Following people around your scene

Premiere Elements comes bundled with nearly 300 pieces of Clip Art – cartoons and graphics that you can use to enhance your movies.

These clips have transparent backgrounds, so you can lay them right onto your videos. And several of them are even animated.

Using Motion Tracking, you can set clip art, graphics and even thought and speech bubbles to follow people in your videos around a scene!

A little-noticed feature in Premiere Elements is its amazing collection of clip art and graphics. These graphic elements are accessed by clicking the **Graphics** button on the far right of the **Toolbar**. (If your computer monitor isn't wide enough to display this button, click the > button on the interface's lower right corner)

Premiere Elements includes nearly 300 graphics in 13 categories, including cartoons, household objects, toys, clothing, speech and thought bubbles and animations. These animations range from the silly (a smiling or frowning face) to quite realistic (including fire, smoke, steam, birds and a butterfly).

These graphics all include alpha or transparent backgrounds, so when you drop them onto your video, they appear as an overlay, incorporated naturally into your movie.

In this chapter we'll look at not only applying these graphics to our video, but we'll also look at customizing them and applying motion paths to them so that they become integrated into the action of a scene.

In *Cool Trick 42*, for instance, we'll place a simple graphic onto a person's face and then follow him with it throughout the scene.

Then, in *Cool Trick 43*, we'll add and customize a speech or thought bubble.

And finally, in *Cool Trick 44*, we'll link text to a moving background so that it stays locked to a stationary object as we drive by.

HOT TIP
What is an alpha channel?

As you likely already know, every color in your videos is composed of a combination of three primary colors: red, green and blue. These three colors bring their video information in as channels, each providing video data for every pixel of every frame in one of 256 levels of color (so that the three channels combine to produce over 16 million colors).

Many video formats, however, include the ability to carry additional information on additional channels – the most common of which is called the alpha channel. This alpha channel provides video data, just as the red, green and blue channels do. However, this information comes in the form of transparency.

In other words, when a video clip includes an alpha channel, a video editing program like Premiere Elements reads it as transparent, revealing the video on the lower video tracks through it. A video of a bird, for instance, that includes an alpha channel can be placed on top of a video of the sky so that the bird video (which includes no background of its own) appears to be flying in the sky.

The graphics that are included with Premiere Elements come in two formats – animated SWF and stationary PNG files – both of which include alpha channels so that they can be overlaid onto your video.

COOL TRICK
42 Follow a Moving Person with a Graphic

Creating a **Motion Tracking** effect involves three basic steps:

1. Identify a person or object in your clip.

2. Generate a motion track to follow that person or object.

3. Link a graphic to that motion track so that it follows the person or object around the scene.

Adobe has designed this tool to be relatively intuitive, so most of the hard work is handled automatically by the tool itself.

1   Select a clip on your timeline

The key to successfully using this tool is having a clip with consistent, even lighting and having a person or object that is distinct enough from the background for the program to clearly identify this target as he, she or it moves around your video frame.

Make sure the **CTI** playhead is positioned at the point in the clip at which you'd like your **Motion Tracking** to begin.

HOT TIP
How does Motion Tracking work?

When you use Premiere Elements' **Motion Tracking** tool to identify a person or object in a clip, the program will do an analysis of the clip and record all of that object's movements within the video frame as **Motion Track** keyframes.

When you link a graphic or text to that **Motion Track**, Premiere Elements will paste those **Motion** keyframes to your graphic's properties.

If you select the graphic on your timeline and click the **Applied Effects** button, you will even be able to see the graphic's keyframes under the **Motion** listing. (You may need to click on the **Show Keyframes** button [the stopwatch] in the upper right of the panel to open the panel's timeline.)

As with any keyframes, these **Motion/Position** keyframes can be adjusted, moved, removed and even added to as necessary to fine tune your graphic's movement over your clip. In some cases, you may even want to enhance your motion track by creating keyframes for **Scale** so that the graphic's size changes over the course of the motion path to match changes in relative size of the tracked object.)

Follow a Moving Person with a Graphic

1. Select the clip you want to track on your timeline.

2. Select Motion Tracking from the Tools.

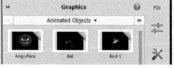

3. On the Motion Tracking Screen, click Select Object and position the box around the object or person you want to track.

4. Click Track Object. The program will track the object from this point until the object becomes unrecognizable.

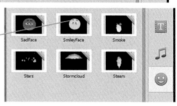

5. Select a graphic from the Graphics collection and drag it onto the the selected object. Position it as needed.

The object will automatically follow the object's motion across your video frame!

2   Launch the Motion Tracking tool

Click on the **Tools** button on the **Toolbar** along the bottom of the program and, from the **Video** toolset, select **Motion Tracking**.

The **Motion Tracking** workspace will open.

3   Indicate the object to be tracked

Click the **Select Object** button in the **Motion Tracking** workspace.

A box with four corner handles will appear in the center of the **Monitor**.

Drag on this box's corner handles so that it surrounds the person or object in your video frame that you'd like to track. For best results, this object's color (or the clothes that the person is wearing) should be distinct enough in color from the rest of the scene so that the program can easily identify this object as it moves.

4   Track the object

Click the **Track Object** button. The program will analyze the clip and create a motion track for the object you have identified. This tracking will begin at the point in your clip at which you've identified your object and will end at either the end of your clip or at the point it no longer recognizes the object it is tracking.

Once it's finished, if you "scrub" the clip (manually dragging the **CTI** playhead through it) the yellow tracking box should follow your person or object.

5   Link a graphic, title or PiP to your motion track

Click on the **Graphics** on the program's **Toolbar**.

Premiere Elements 2018 includes over 300 "clip art" images – many of them animated. These images are ideal for linking to a motion track. (The animated clips are particularly fun to use.)

You aren't limited to linking your tracked object to clip art, however. By dragging a clip or still from your **Project Assets** (which, in the **Motion Tracking** workspace is in the upper *right* of the program's interface) you can create a **Picture-in-Picture** that follows your tracked object – and, if you've created a title prior to opening the Motion Tracking tool, you can also drag it from **Project Assets** and this text will follow your object (as we show you in *Cool Trick 44*.

Once your graphic appears in the **Monitor,** you can drag it to any position, relative to the **Motion Tracking Object** box and your tracked object.

By dragging in and out on the graphic's corner handles, you can scale its size.

Note that the graphic you've added will also on your timeline as a clip on a video track above the video you are tracking.

HOT TIP
Additional content

You may notice a little blue flag over the upper right corner of a number of templates and graphics in Premiere Elements.

This blue flag indicates that the template or theme is available but has not yet been installed on your computer.

SadFace

Speech Bubble

The first time you select this template or add graphic to your movie, the program will automatically download it for you from the Adobe site – a process that should only take a moment or two. Once you've downloaded it, it will always be readily available.

If you'd like to download all of the program's templates at once, **right-click** on any one of these templates or graphics and select the **Download All** option.

As with any graphic, you can drag on the end of the clip on the timeline to extend its duration so that it remains on-screen for your entire **Motion Track** sequence. (Note that **Animated Clip Art** images, however, have a fixed maximum length – so they can be trimmed shorter but not extended beyond their animation's duration.)

By the way, you are not limited to linking a single graphic to **Motion Track**. You can link several graphics to a single **Motion Tracking Object**.

Likewise, you can add more than one **Motion Tracking Object** to a single clip. Each **Motion Track Object** you add will be indicated with a yellow box when your **Monitor** is in **Motion Tracking Mode**. The **Motion Tracking Object** you have selected at the time (It will be blue while the unselected **Object boxes** will remain yellow) is the motion track that the clip art or graphic you add will be linked to.

To delete a **Motion Track**, select the **Motion Tracking** tool and, in the **Motion Tracking** workspace, **right-click** on the yellow **Motion Tracking** box and select the option to **Delete Selected Object**.

COOL TRICK

43 Add a Thought or Speech Bubble to Your Movie

In addition to still graphics and animated clips, Premiere Elements' **Graphics** collection includes a number of cartoon thought and speech bubbles, the text of which can be customized and edited.

And, as with any clips or graphics linked to a **Motion Tracking Object**, these thought and speech bubbles will follow a person, object – or even a pet around your video frame!

1 **Select a clip on your timeline**

The key to successfully using this tool is having a clip with consistent, even lighting and having a person or object that is distinct enough from the background for the program to clearly identify this target as he, she or it moves around your video frame.

Make sure the **CTI** playhead is positioned at the point in the clip at which you'd like your **Motion Tracking** to begin.

2 **Launch the Motion Tracking tool**

Click on the **Tools** button on the **Toolbar** along the bottom of the program and, from the **Video** toolset, select **Motion Tracking**.

The **Motion Tracking** workspace will open.

3 **Indicate the object to be tracked**

Click the **Select Object** button.

A box with four corner handles will appear in the center of the **Monitor**.

Add a Speech or Thought Bubble to Your Movie
(Part 1)

1. Select the clip you want to track on your timeline.

2. Select Motion Tracking from the Tools.

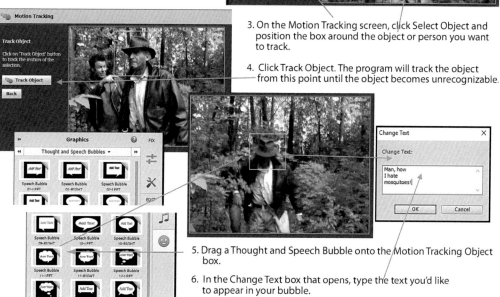

3. On the Motion Tracking screen, click Select Object and position the box around the object or person you want to track.

4. Click Track Object. The program will track the object from this point until the object becomes unrecognizable.

5. Drag a Thought and Speech Bubble onto the Motion Tracking Object box.

6. In the Change Text box that opens, type the text you'd like to appear in your bubble.

Drag on this box's corner handles so that it indicates the person or object in your video frame that you'd like to track. For best results, this object's color (or the clothes that the person is wearing) should be distinct enough in color from the rest of the scene so that the program can easily identify this object as it moves.

4 Track the object

Click the **Track Object** button. The program will analyze the clip and create a motion track for the object you have identified. This tracking will begin at the point in your clip at which you've identified your object and will end at either the end of your clip or at the point it no longer recognizes the object it's tracking.

Once it's finished, if you "scrub" the clip (manually dragging the **CTI** playhead through it) you should see the yellow tracking box follow your person or object.

5 **Link a Thought or Speech Bubble**

While remaining in the **Motion Tracking** workspace, click on the **Graphics** button on the program's **Toolbar**.

Browse to the **Thought & Speech Bubbles** category of graphics. Select and drag a thought or speech bubble onto the **Motion Tracking Box** on your **Monitor**.

6 **Add custom text**

When you place a **Thought or Speech Bubble** onto your **Monitor** panel, a **Change Text** option box will appear.

Type in your custom text and click **OK**.

Don't be concerned if your text seems to run outside of the **Thought or Speech Bubble**. We'll fix that in a moment.

Once your **Thought or Speech Bubble** appears in the **Monitor**, you can drag it to any position, relative to the **Motion Tracking Object** box and your tracked object.

By dragging in and out on the **Thought or Speech Bubble's** corner handles, you can scale its size.

Scrub through the clips on your timeline (by dragging the **CTI** playhead) to ensure that Premiere Elements has created the motion path for the graphic that follows your **Motion Tracking Object**. If necessary, drag the end(s) of the thought or speech clip (on Video 2) to extend or shorten its duration.

7 **Open the Thought of Speech Bubble for editing**

Your **Thought or Speech Bubble** will appear as a clip on your timeline on a video track above the clip you are **Motion Tracking**.

HOT TIP
Thought and Speech Bubbles are title templates

Thought and speech bubbles are essentially **Title & Text** templates – and, when you open then in the **Title Adjustments** workspace, they can be edited exactly the same way.

On the **Text Adjustments** tab, you'll find tools to customize the font, text color, size and alignment. If you switch from the **Type** to the **Selection Tool**, you change the position or size of the text or any graphics on the title.

On the **Style** tab, you'll find options for applying a font and color style to your text.

On the **Animation** tab, you'll find tools for applying an incoming or outgoing animation to your title.

On the **Shapes** tab, you can create additional graphics for your title – or select and delete existing graphics.

Add a Speech or Thought Bubble to Your Movie (Part 2)

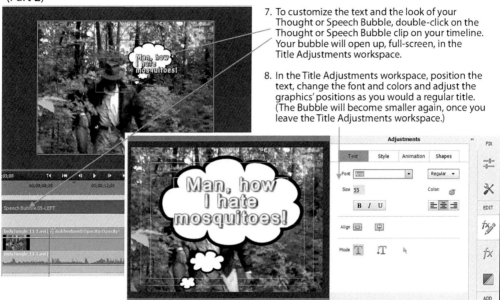

7. To customize the text and the look of your Thought or Speech Bubble, double-click on the Thought or Speech Bubble clip on your timeline. Your bubble will open up, full-screen, in the Title Adjustments workspace.

8. In the Title Adjustments workspace, position the text, change the font and colors and adjust the graphics' positions as you would a regular title. (The Bubble will become smaller again, once you leave the Title Adjustments workspace.)

This clip is essentially a title clip, and can be edited in the **Titles** workspace.

Double-click on the **Thought or Speech Bubble** clip on your timeline.

Your bubble will open in the **Title Adjustments** workspace.

Although your **Thought or Speech Bubble** will also appear full-screen while you are in the **Titles** workspace, when you return to video editing mode it will again become a smaller graphic, linked to your **Motion Tracking Object**.

8   Edit your Thought or Speech Bubble

When you have the **Type Tool** selected (the "T" on the **Titles Toolbar** on the upper right of the **Monitor** panel), you can select and edit the text or apply text styles or animation.

When the **Selection Tool** is selected (the arrow on the **Text** tab), you can adjust the positions of the elements in the title, including the text.

By dragging in or out on the corner handles for the text block or "bubble" graphics, you can resize it.

To return Premiere Elements to video editing mode, click to select one of the clips on your timeline.

If the object or person you're linking your **Thought or Speech Bubble** to is moving, the graphic will follow its movement around your video frame.

44 Lock a Title to a Background in Motion

Just as you can link a graphic or clip so that it follows a person or object as it moves around your video frame, you can use the **Motion Tracking** tool to lock a graphic, clip or a title so that it stays in position on your background as your camera moves or changes position.

In this **Cool Trick**, we'll take a clip of a video shot while driving down a street, and we'll link a title to a parked car in the shot so that the title will remain in position, relative to the car, even as it moves left and out of the video frame.

1 Create a title

Because you can't have the **Title Adjustments** workspace and the **Motion Tracking** workspace open at the same time, we'll first need to create a title and then delete it from our timeline so that we'll have it in our **Project Assets** when we do our **Motion Tracking**.

From the **Text** menu at the top of the program, select **New Title/Default Text**. A generic title will be added to your timeline and the **Title Adjustments** workspace will open.

Overwrite the placeholder text with your own text and customize its look. Click on the timeline to leave the **Title Adjustments** workspace.

2 Delete your title clip from the timeline

Your new title will appear as a clip on your timeline. Select it and press the **Delete** key on your keyboard. (Or, to avoid any timeline rippling that could change the positions of your other clips, **right-click** on the title clip on your timeline and select **Delete**.)

Although your title will disappear from the timeline, it will remain as a clip in your **Project Assets**.

3 Launch the Motion Tracking tool

Select the video clip you'd like to apply to attach your title to, then click on the **Tools** button on the **Toolbar** along the bottom of the program and, from the **Video** toolset, select **Motion Tracking**.

The **Motion Tracking** workspace will open.

4 Indicate the object to be tracked

Click the **Select Object** button.

A box with four corner handles will appear in the center of the **Monitor**.

Drag on this box's corner handles so that it indicates the person or object in your video frame that you'd like to track. For best results, this object's color (or the clothes that the person is wearing) should be distinct enough in color from the rest of the scene so that the program can easily identify this object as it moves.

Lock a Title to a Moving Background

1. Add a title to your timeline by selecting Default Text from the program's Text menu and customize it in the Title Adjustments workspace.

2. Delete the title from your timeline – though it will remain in your Project Assets.

3. Select Motion tracking from the Tools menu on the Action Bar.

4. Indicate the object or scenery you want to lock to.

5. Click Track Object to follow its motion across your video frame.

6. Drag your title from the Project Assets (in the upper right of the workspace) onto the Monitor and position it relative to your tracked object.

Your title will lock to the object in your scene, even following it off-screen.

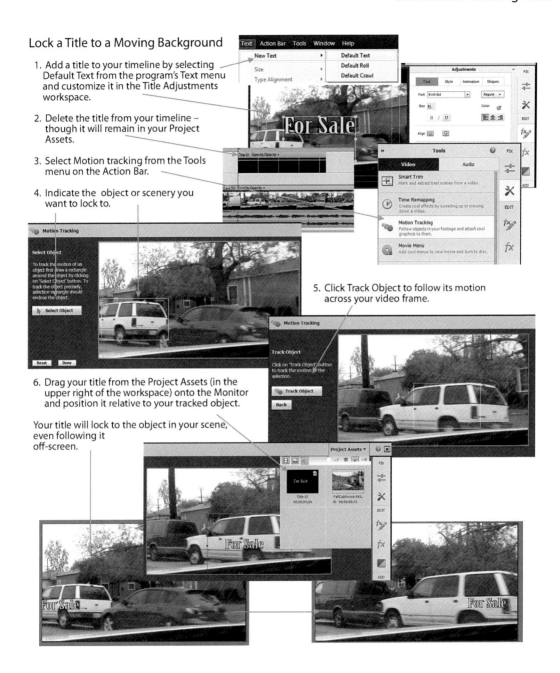

5 **Track the object**

   Click the **Track Object** button. The program will analyze the clip and create a motion track for the object you have identified. This tracking will begin at the point in your clip at which you've identified your object and will end at either the end of your clip or at the point it no longer recognizes the object it is tracking.

Once it's finished, if you "scrub" the clip (manually dragging the **CTI** playhead through it) you should see the yellow tracking box follow your person or object.

6   **Link your title to your motion track**

Open your **Project Media** by clicking on the tab that, in this workspace, in the upper *right* of the program.

Drag your title from **Project Assets** media panel onto the yellow **Motion Tracking Object Selection Box** in clip in **Monitor** panel.

When you release your mouse button, you'll be given the option of revising your title's text. Click **OK**.

Once your title appears in the **Monitor**, you can drag it to any position, relative to the **Motion Tracking Object** box and your tracked object.

By dragging in and out on the title's corner handles, you can scale its size.

Click **Done** to leave the **Motion Tracking** workspace.

Play your clip or scrub through it (by dragging the **CTI** playhead) to ensure that your title indeed tracks with the movement of your **Motion Tracking Object** across the video frame.

Play your clip or scrub through it (by dragging the **CTI** playhead) to ensure that your graphic or title stays with the object you're tracking the whole way across the video frame.

If necessary, you can add more keyframes between these initial and final keyframes so that the title stays in precise position over the object. To do so, position the **CTI** at the point at which you need to make your adjustment and then drag the title into position on the **Monitor** panel. New keyframes will automatically be created at the **CTI's** position.

In my example, the car in the video that I've linked my title to actually goes off the side of the screen. Because the **Motion Tracking** tool will not follow on object off-screen, I've added some addition **Motion** keyframes to the title so that the title continues to follow the car even as it disappears off the edge of the video frame (as we did in *Cool Trick 5*).

Ideally, the effect should appear as if the title or graphic is actually a part of the scenery – and we're driving past it!

Chapter 13
Cool Map Tricks
Taking your viewer on a journey

Maps can greatly enhance your videos.

Using maps, you can orient your audience – show them where in the world your story takes place (or where your vacation took you).

And a good, interesting, moving map can add a classic, Indiana Jones-style look to your video.

Maps are great tools for helping orient your audience as to where things happened and how you got there. And that's true whether you're telling an adventure story or just recounting your family trip.

Adding motion to a map makes it all the more interesting. An animated map can show the routes you traveled – and, to make it more interesting, you can even add a model of the vehicle you took to get there!

Here are three classic map tricks, each building on the effect created in the *Cool Trick* before it.

45 Add a Moving Line to a Map

This is the classic map animation – and it's remarkably simple, using a couple of basic keyframing tricks.

Using the **Crop** tool and then keyframing the motion of the **Crop** to reveal one map image over another, we'll create the illusion of a red line being drawn across our map.

To create this effect, you'll need two images:

- A map image.
- A copy of that image, but with a red line on it tracing your route.

Remember, by the way, that most maps are copyrighted material. So ensure that you either secure the necessary rights and/or give the necessary credit if you use any map image (even the ubiquitous Google Maps) in any work you plan to release to the public.

As an alternative, you can create your own map, using an existing map as a reference.

1 **Place your Map clip on Video 1**

Drag the Map clip from your **Project Assets** panel to the Video 1 track.

2 **Place Map_w_Line on Video 2**

Drag the map image with the line drawn over it (Map_w_Line) from your **Project Assets** panel to the Video 2 track, directly over the Map clip, as illustrated on page 174.

Because we aren't doing any Motion keyframing in this *Cool Trick*, if your images are larger than a standard video frame, right-click on each clip and select the option to **Scale to Frame** Size.

By default, still photos and graphics are five seconds long. If you'd like to extend the length of these clips – and, hence, extend the length of this effect – you can do so by dragging the end of the clip(s) on your timeline to extend their duration.

3   **Locate the Crop effect**

Click the **Effects** button on the program's **Toolbar**.

The **Crop** effect is located in the **Transform** category of **Video Effects**.

HOT TIP
Sizing your graphics to fit your video frame

At Muvipix.com, we recommend that, for best performance with Premiere Elements, you always work with graphics and photos that are optimally size. For most graphics and photos to be used in standard definition video, this size is 1000x750 pixels (at 72 ppi). At 1000x750 pixels, your image will be large enough to allow for some panning and zooming and yet not so large that it will bog down the program.

When working with 1920x1080 high-definition video, the optimal size for your photos and graphics is 2500x1875 pixels (at 72 ppi). (Though also note our *Hot Tip* on page 44.)

When you are using an image that large in your Premiere Elements project, there are two ways to size it so that it fits your video frame.

- The easiest way to *automatically* scale your graphic to fit your video frame is to right-click on it on your timeline and select **Scale to Frame Size**. However, although this will automatically size your image, this method also limits some of the other things you can do with your graphic, including motion path keyframing.

- The preferred **manual** method of sizing your image is to select the clip on your timeline and click the **Applied Effects** button on the right side of the program. This will open the clip's **Applied Effects** panel. Click on the **Motion** listing to open its properties and settings, then set **Scale** of a 1000x750 image to 65% for a standard definition project or set the **Scale** of a 2500x1875 image to 95% for high-def. This scales the image to fit your video frame and still leaves the option of creating **Scale** and **Position** motion path keyframes at a later time, if you'd like.

If you have two, virtually identical graphics (such as the Map and Map_w_Line graphics we use in *Cool Trick 45*, you can ensure that they are identically scaled and positioned in your video frame using the **Paste Effects and Adjustments** feature.

To use it, set the **Scale** and **Position** of one clip so that it is properly positioned in your **Monitor**. Right-click on this clip on your timeline and select **Copy**, then right-click on the second clip and select **Paste Effects and Adjustments**. The identical **Scale** and **Position** (as well as any other effects, motion paths or keyframing) will be applied to both clips!

Add a Moving Line to a Map

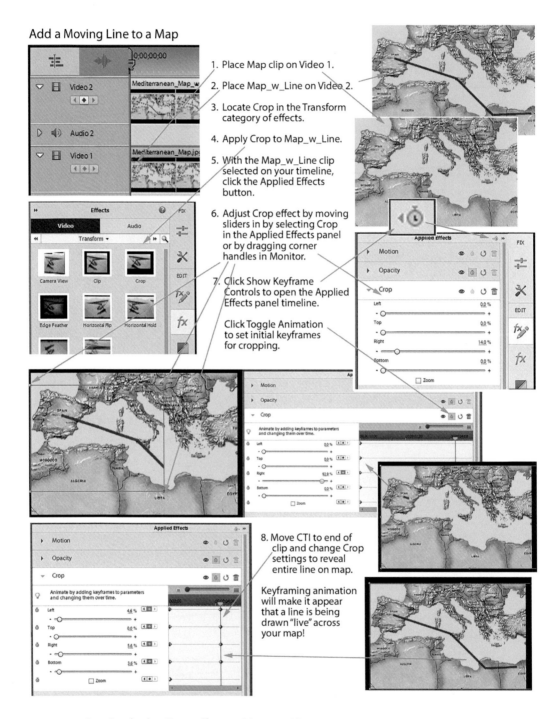

1. Place Map clip on Video 1.

2. Place Map_w_Line on Video 2.

3. Locate Crop in the Transform category of effects.

4. Apply Crop to Map_w_Line.

5. With the Map_w_Line clip selected on your timeline, click the Applied Effects button.

6. Adjust Crop effect by moving sliders in by selecting Crop in the Applied Effects panel or by dragging corner handles in Monitor.

7. Click Show Keyframe Controls to open the Applied Effects panel timeline.

   Click Toggle Animation to set initial keyframes for cropping.

8. Move CTI to end of clip and change Crop settings to reveal entire line on map.

   Keyframing animation will make it appear that a line is being drawn "live" across your map!

4 Apply the Crop effect to Map_w_Line

Select the Map_w_Line clip on your timeline and drag the **Crop** effect onto it.

The **Crop** effect will be applied to your clip, but at its default settings – which will mean that your line will appear somewhat randomly cropped, if at all.

5   Open the Map_w_Line's Applied Effects panel

With the Map_w_Line clip selected on your timeline, click the **Applied Effects** button on the right side of the program.

The clip's **Applied Effects** panel will open.

6   Adjust the Crop effect

Click on the **Crop** listing in the **Applied Effects** panel to open the effect's properties and settings.

The **Crop** effect's properties settings consist of four sliders, each representing a side of your image and a percentage of that side which the **Crop** effect will trim off.

Because the **Crop** effect trims off the sides of your image and thus reveals the image on the track below, you may need to play with these sliders a bit to get a feel for how they will trim away at the sides of your Map_w_Line graphic.

Because your image on the Video 2 track is identical to the image on the Video 1 track (except for the red line), **cropping Map_w_Line will appear to merely be trimming or adding the red line.**

And that is exactly the effect we want!

Move the sliders to crop Map_w_Line back to the very beginning of your travel route. (As an alternative to using the sliders to set your crop, you can click to select the **Crop** effect in the **Applied Effects** panel and then drag the corner handles that appear in your **Monitor** panel.)

It's important to think ahead as you crop. Try to imagine how this cropping is going to "un-crop" to create the illusion of your line being drawn over the course of this sequence.

If, for instance, your line runs almost directly north, south, east or west, you may be best cropping only one side of your Map_w_Line image. (In my case, my route of travel is almost directly from west to east, so I'll be keyframing my animation almost exclusively with the **Right** side settings.) If your line is curved or angled, you may need to combine animations of two sides of the cropping to get the effect of a smooth line of travel.

7   Set an initial Crop keyframe.

Click on the **Show Keyframe Controls** button (the stopwatch) in the upper right of the **Applied Effects** panel to open the panel's timeline.

Move the **CTI** playhead to the beginning of the clip or the point in the clip that you'd like your animation to begin.

Click the **Toggle Animation** button (the stopwatch) to the right of the **Crop** listing in the **Applied Effects** panel.

A set of initial keyframe points will appear on the **Applied Effects** panel timeline at the position of the **CTI**.

8   Create the final Crop keyframe(s)

Drag your **CTI** to the position at which you'd like your red line to finish being drawn.

Adjust your cropping (either by moving the sliders or by clicking on the **Crop** effect listing in the **Applied Effects** panel and dragging on the corner handles that appear on the **Monitor**) to reveal the entire red line.

As you change the positions of any side's cropping, new keyframe points will automatically be added to the **Applied Effects** panel timeline at the position of the **CTI**.

How much tweaking you have to do – and how many more keyframes you need to add along the way – depends on how complicated your red line is. The more turns it makes, the more keyframe points you'll have to add along the way to follow it.

It can also be challenging to give your animation a smooth, even pace. But remember how keyframes work. The closer they are together, the faster the animation. So pacing your animation is as simple as adjusting the positions of the keyframe points on your **Applied Effects** panel timeline.

COOL TRICK

46 Add a Moving Line to a Moving Map

This effect takes the effect we created in *Cool Trick 45* one step further. This time out, instead of just adding a moving line to a map, we'll make the map move too!

In other words, we're going to be simultaneously running two keyframing effects – one of which creates the animation of a line being drawn across a map and the other of which creates a pan and zoom motion path over the map.

As in *Cool Trick 45*, we'll need two image files:

- A map image.
- A copy of that image, but with a red line on it tracing your route.

And, *before* you add import images into your project, make sure you go to the program's **Preferences** (under the **Edit** menu on a PC) and, on the **General** page, *uncheck* the option to **Default Scale to Frame Size**. When checked, this feature can make creating motion paths with photos and graphics very difficult.

1   Place your Map clip on Video 1

Drag the Map clip from your **Project Assets** panel to the Video 1 track.

Add a Moving Line to a Moving Map (Part 1)

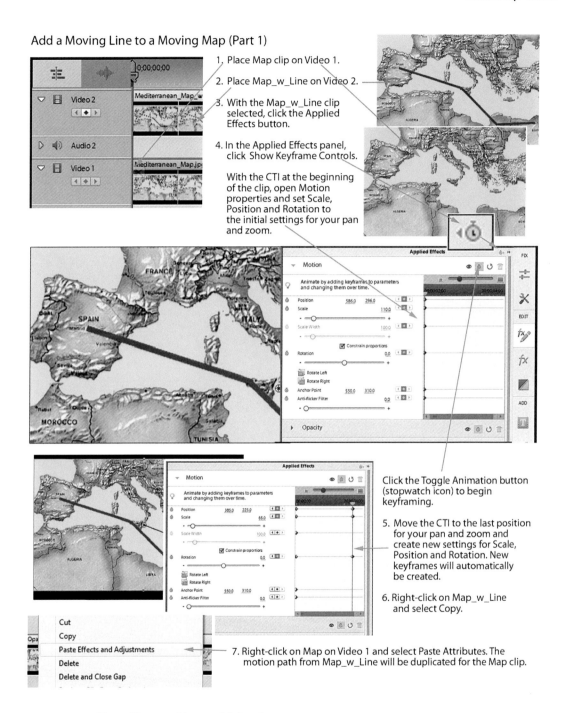

1. Place Map clip on Video 1.

2. Place Map_w_Line on Video 2.

3. With the Map_w_Line clip selected, click the Applied Effects button.

4. In the Applied Effects panel, click Show Keyframe Controls.

   With the CTI at the beginning of the clip, open Motion properties and set Scale, Position and Rotation to the initial settings for your pan and zoom.

Click the Toggle Animation button (stopwatch icon) to begin keyframing.

5. Move the CTI to the last position for your pan and zoom and create new settings for Scale, Position and Rotation. New keyframes will automatically be created.

6. Right-click on Map_w_Line and select Copy.

7. Right-click on Map on Video 1 and select Paste Attributes. The motion path from Map_w_Line will be duplicated for the Map clip.

2   Place Map_w_Line on Video 2

Drag the map image with the line drawn over it (Map_w_Line) from your **Project Assets** panel to the Video 2 track, directly over the Map clip.

By default, still photos and graphics are five seconds long. If you'd like to extend the length of these clips – and, hence, extend the length of this effect – you can do so by dragging the end of the clip(s) to extend their duration.

3   Open the Map_w_Line's Applied Effects panel

Select the Map_w_Line clip on your timeline and click the **Applied Effects** button the right side of the program.

The **Applied Effects** panel for this clip will open.

4   Create an initial Motion keyframe for Map_w_Line

Click on the **Motion** listing in the **Applied Effects** panel to open its properties and settings.

Click the **Show Keyframe Controls** button (the stopwatch) in the upper right of the panel to open the **Applied Effects** panel timeline.

Ensure that the **CTI** playhead is at the beginning of your clip.

Set the initial position of your pan and zoom effect by adjusting **Scale, Position** and/or **Rotation**.

Effects and properties can be set in a number of ways. In the **Applied Effects** panel, you can adjust the sliders or type in settings manually. But many people find the most intuitive way to adjust many effects and properties (including **Scale, Position** and **Rotation**) is to click to select the effect listing in the **Applied Effects** panel (in this case, **Motion**) and then dragging on the corner handles that frame your clip in the **Monitor** panel.

Once you've set the initial position for your pan and zoom on Map_ w_Line, click the **Toggle Animation** (stopwatch) button to the right of the **Motion** listing to begin your keyframing session.

A set of diamond-shaped keyframes will appear for each of the **Motion** properties on the **Applied Effects** panel timeline at the position of the **CTI**.

5   Create a final Motion keyframe for Map_w_Line

Move the **CTI** to the end of the clip on the **Applied Effects** panel timeline or to the position in the clip at which you'd like your pan and zoom motion path over the map to end.

Set your **Scale, Position** and/or **Rotation** to the final position for your pan and zoom either by using the sliders, typing the settings in numerically or by clicking on the **Motion** listing in the **Applied Effects** panel and dragging on the corner handles for the clip in the **Monitor.**

New keyframe points will automatically be added at the position of the **CTI**.

We've just created a motion path pan and zoom for the Map_w_Line image, as we did in *Cool Trick 10*. It's a good idea to play it back and give it a test drive and see if it's the movement and pacing you want before we go any further. (You may need to render it, by pressing the **Enter** key on your keyboard, before you play back your clip to see it at full quality.)

Add or adjust the **Motion** keyframes if you'd like. But try to get it as close to final as you can. This aspect of your effect won't be so easy to change later.

6 **Copy the keyframing from Map_w_Line**

   Right-click on Map_w_Line on your timeline and select **Copy**.

   This will copy all of the effects (including the keyframed pan and zoom path) which have been applied to this clip.

7 **Paste Effects and Adjustments to Map**

   Right-click on the Map clip on Video 1 and select **Paste Effects and Adjustments**.

   All of the effects and animations from Map_w_Line will be applied to the Map clip – lining them up in the video frame and synchronizing their pan and zoom movements!

In other words, at this point the Map clip on the Video 1 track and the Map_w_Line clip on the Video 2 track are panning and zooming in perfect sync.

Now we'll add to the Map_w_Line clip essentially the same keyframed **Crop** effect as we did in *Cool Trick 45* – but this time revealing the red line across the map at the same time as we pan and zoom over the map!

8 **Locate the Crop effect**

   Click the **Effects** button on the program's **Toolbar**.

   The **Crop** effect is located in the **Transform** category of **Video Effects**.

9 **Apply the Crop effect to Map_w_Line**

   Select the Map_w_Line clip on your timeline and drag the **Crop** effect onto it.

   The **Crop** effect will be applied to your clip, but at its default settings – which will mean that your line will appear somewhat randomly cropped, if at all.

10 **Open the Map_w_Line's Applied Effects panel**

   With the Map_w_Line clip selected on your timeline, click the **Applied Effects** button on the right side of the program.

Add a Moving Line to a Moving Map (Part 2)

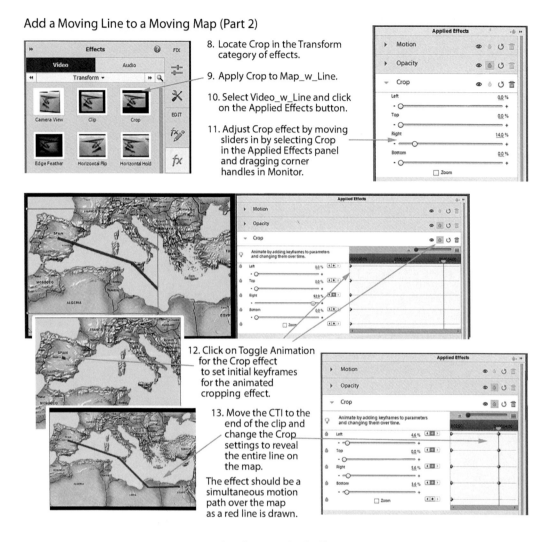

8. Locate Crop in the Transform category of effects.

9. Apply Crop to Map_w_Line.

10. Select Video_w_Line and click on the Applied Effects button.

11. Adjust Crop effect by moving sliders in by selecting Crop in the Applied Effects panel and dragging corner handles in Monitor.

12. Click on Toggle Animation for the Crop effect to set initial keyframes for the animated cropping effect.

13. Move the CTI to the end of the clip and change the Crop settings to reveal the entire line on the map.

The effect should be a simultaneous motion path over the map as a red line is drawn.

The clip's **Applied Effects** panel will open.

11 Adjust the Crop effect

Click on the **Crop** listing in the **Applied Effects** panel to open the effect's properties and settings.

The **Crop** effect's properties settings consist of four sliders, each representing a side of your image and a percentage of that side which the **Crop** effect will trim off.

Because the **Crop** effect trims off the sides of your image and thus reveals the image on the track below, you may need to play with these sliders a bit to get a feel for how they will trim away at the sides of your Map_w_Line graphic.

Because our image on the Video 2 track is identical to the image on the Video 1 track (except for the red line), cropping

Map_w_Line will actually appear to merely be trimming the red line.

And that is exactly the effect we want!

Move the sliders to crop Map_w_Line back to the very beginning of your travel route. (As an alternative to using the sliders to set your crop, you can click to select the **Crop** effect in the **Applied Effects** panel and then drag the corner handles that appear in your **Monitor** panel.)

It's important to think ahead as you crop. Try to imagine how this cropping is going to "un-crop" to create the illusion of your line being drawn over the course of this sequence.

If, for instance, your line runs almost directly north, south, east or west, you may be best cropping only one side of your Map_w_Line image. (In my case, my route of travel is almost directly from west to east, so I'll be keyframing my animation almost exclusively with the **Right** side settings.)

HOT TIP
Simplifying the process of adding multiple keyframed effects

Although you can add as many effects as you'd like to a clip – and you can even have several sets of keyframed effects running at once – you may find it a bit challenging to keep them all moving relative to each other. In *Cool Trick 46* and *Cool Trick 47,* for instance, you may find it difficult to create a smooth, evenly-paced line drawing animation while your motion path is panning and zooming around your image.

You may find it easier to add your keyframed effects one at a time. You can do this by outputting each of your keyframed motion path sequences as a separate video file and then applying your **Crop** effect keyframing to the new video clips you've output.

For instance:

1. Create a motion path pan and zoom over your Map_w_Line.

    If you're working in standard definition video, output the clip by going to **Export & Share/Devices/Computer** and selecting the option for a **720x480 AVI** or **MOV**. Duplicate this motion path for the Map clip using **Paste Adjustments and Effects** (as described in *Cool Trick 46*, **Step 6** and **Step 7**) and output this sequence also.

    For AVCHD high-definition video, output each video segment by going to **Export & Share/Devices/Computer** and selecting the option for a **1920x1080 MP4**.

2. Use **Add Media/Files and Folders** to browse to these new video clips and add them to your project. Place each clip on your timeline (in place of your previously created motion clips) and keyframe the **Crop** effect as described in *Cool Trick 45*.

12 **Set an initial Crop keyframe.**

Click on the **Show Keyframe Controls** button (the stopwatch) in the upper right of the **Applied Effects** panel to open the panel's timeline.

Move the **CTI** playhead to the beginning of the clip or the point in the clip that you'd like your animation to begin.

Click the **Toggle Animation** button (the stopwatch) to the right of the **Crop** listing in the **Applied Effects** panel.

A set of initial keyframe points will appear on the **Applied Effects** panel timeline at the position of the **CTI**.

13 **Create the final Crop keyframe(s)**

Drag your **CTI** to the position at which you'd like your red line to finish being drawn.

Adjust your cropping (either by moving the sliders or by clicking on the **Crop** effect listing in the **Applied Effects** panel and dragging on the corner handles that appear on the **Monitor**) to reveal the entire red line.

As you change the positions of any side's cropping, new keyframe points will automatically be added to the **Applied Effects** panel timeline at the position of the **CTI**.

Because you are chasing two sets of keyframed animation at a time, it can take some tweaking to get the **Crop** effect to work smoothly at the same time as the motion path is panning and zooming – but the results will definitely be worth it!

COOL TRICK
47 Add a Car or Airplane to Your Moving Line

This effect takes the effects we created in *Cool Trick 45* and *Cool Trick 46* one step further. This time out, in addition to adding a moving line to a map, we'll include a graphic: a car or an airplane that tracks along that moving line.

Creating the effect is pretty simple really. We'll just add the graphic on an upper video track and then keyframe the motion to follow the moving line. Creating the graphic for the car or the airplane can present some challenges, however. This is because most graphics that you use in Premiere Elements are square or rectangular – the shape of what Photoshop Elements calls the "canvas," or the image background.

But we don't want our car or airplane to be on a square background! We want our graphic to be shaped like a car or an airplane. We, then, will need to create a graphic with no background and then save it in a graphics file format that displays the area around our graphic as transparent.

HOT TIP
Create a non-square graphic in Photoshop Elements

Most graphics you use are square or rectangular. However, you often have the need for graphics that are non-square or irregular shaped – such as the car, airplane or other vehicle you will use in *Cool Trick 47.*

There are two things you must do to create a non-square graphic:

- You must remove the **Background** from the image or convert the **Background** into a layer and remove the areas you want to make transparent.

- You must save your graphic in a format that supports transparency. The ideal format for preserving transparency is the PSD file, the native file format for Photoshop and Photoshop Elements.

To turn a square graphic into a non-square graphic:

1 Open the image file or photograph in Photoshop Elements

It doesn't matter what file format you begin with.

Double-click on the Background in the Layers panel.

Click OK on the option panel.

2 Convert the Background into a layer

Double-click on the **Background** layer on the **Layers** panel. An option panel will open asking you to name the layer. You can name your layer or just click okay and accept the default name.

Your Background will become a floating layer with no Background.

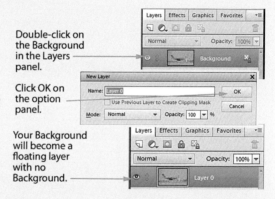

3. Remove the non-essential imagery

If your image appears with a white or other single-color background, you can select the **Magic Wand** tool from the **Toolbox** along the left side of the Photoshop Elements editor workspace and just click to select the background. Otherwise, you'll have to manually select the areas you want removed using one of the selection tools.

As you select and delete areas of your file, a gray checkerboard will indicate areas that are transparent.

When you press the **Delete** key on your keyboard, the selected areas will be removed.

You can also use the **Eraser Tool** to remove unwanted imagery from your file.

The gray checkerboard you see through your graphic indicates areas that will be transparent when the file is used in Premiere Elements or most other Adobe programs.

4 Save your file as a PSD

The *Hot Tip* on the previous page describes how to create such a graphic in Photoshop Elements. If you are using another graphics program, it likely has a similar system for creating and storing transparency in an image file. If using a program other than Photoshop or Photoshop Elements, save your graphic as a transparent PNG.

Once this semi-transparent graphic is created and saved as a PSD, click on the **Add Media**, then select **Files and Folders**. Browse to your PSD file and import it into your Premiere Elements project.

1   **Create a "Moving Line" effect**

Create a "moving line on a map" effect, as demonstrated in *Cool Trick 45* or *Cool Trick 46*.

We will overlay the motion of our vehicle over this effect.

2   **Add your Vehicle graphic to Video 3**

Drag the non-square graphic of your airplane, car, etc., (Vehicle) from your **Project Assets** panel to the Video 3 track on your timeline, positioned directly above your "moving line" effect.

If necessary, you can extend the duration of this vehicle graphic to match the length of the other clips by clicking and dragging on the clip's end on the timeline.

3   **Open Vehicle's Applied Effects panel**

Select the Vehicle clip on your timeline and click the **Applied Effects** button on the right side of the program.

The selected clip's **Applied Effects** panel will open.

4   **Size and position the Vehicle clip**

Click on the **Motion** listing in the **Applied Effects** panel to open its properties and settings.

Adjust the **Scale** and **Position** of the Vehicle clip so that it is over the starting point for your moving line in your **Monitor** panel. (You can also adjust the **Rotation** so that the vehicle is pointing in the direction it will "move".)

You can set the **Position, Scale** and **Rotation** by moving the sliders or typing in the new settings numerically in the **Applied Effects** panel. Or you can more intuitively change the clip's **Position, Scale** and **Rotation** by clicking to select the **Motion** listing in the **Applied Effects** panel and then dragging on the frame and corner handles that appear around the Vehicle clip in your **Monitor** panel, as in the illustration.

Add a Car or Airplane to Your Moving Line

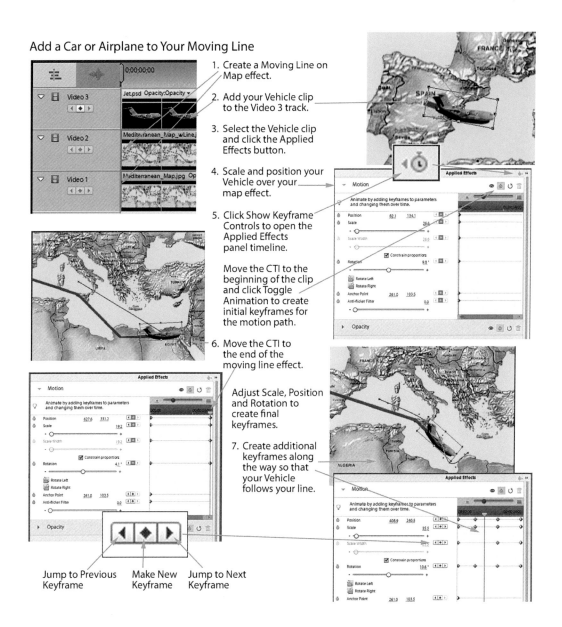

1. Create a Moving Line on Map effect.

2. Add your Vehicle clip to the Video 3 track.

3. Select the Vehicle clip and click the Applied Effects button.

4. Scale and position your Vehicle over your map effect.

5. Click Show Keyframe Controls to open the Applied Effects panel timeline.

   Move the CTI to the beginning of the clip and click Toggle Animation to create initial keyframes for the motion path.

6. Move the CTI to the end of the moving line effect.

   Adjust Scale, Position and Rotation to create final keyframes.

7. Create additional keyframes along the way so that your Vehicle follows your line.

Jump to Previous Keyframe   Make New Keyframe   Jump to Next Keyframe

5   Set the initial keyframes for the Vehicle clip

Click the **Show Keyframe Controls** button (the stopwatch) in the upper right of the panel to open the **Applied Effects** panel timeline.

Move the **CTI** playhead on the **Applied Effects** panel timeline to the beginning of the clip or the point at which you want your effect to begin.

Click the **Toggle Animation** button (the stopwatch icon) to the right of the **Motion** listing in the **Applied Effects** panel. A set of diamond-shaped keyframe points will be added to the **Applied Effects** panel timeline at the position of the **CTI**.

6   Set the final keyframes for the Vehicle clip

Move the **CTI** on the **Applied Effects** panel timeline to the end of the moving line effect.

Drag the Vehicle in the **Monitor** panel, to the end of the line on your map. Change the **Scale** and **Rotation** as necessary, either by dragging on the clip's corner handles or by changing the settings numerically or using the sliders in the **Applied Effects** panel.

New keyframe points will automatically be added at the position of the **CTI** as each setting is changed.

You've now created a direct line from your line's starting point to ending point.

Most likely, though, the line on your map won't follow a straight, direct line. Fortunately, adding additional "waypoints" along the way is easy.

7   Create additional keyframes for your Vehicle clip

The easiest way to figure out where additional keyframes are needed is to "scrub" through your video by dragging the **CTI** playhead over your clip.

HOT TIP
Add depth with a Drop Shadow

If you'd like the car or airplane graphic you've added over your map to stand out, you can add depth to the effect by applying a **Drop Shadow** to the clip.

The **Drop Shadow** effect is located in the **Perspective** category of **Video Effects**.

Once you apply a **Drop Shadow** to your clip, you can tweak the effect in the clip's **Applied Effects** panel. (To open the **Applied Effects** panel, select the clip on your timeline and click the **Applied Effects** button on the right side of the program.)

Shadow Color. To change the color of the **Drop Shadow**, click on the swatch and select a color from the **Color Picker** screen that opens.

Direction. The direction the shadow falls behind your clip is measured in degrees, based on a 360-degree circle. A shadow falling to the rear and left of your clip would set to about 230.

Distance. Sets how far the shadow is separated from your clip.

Softness. A higher setting creates a softer shadow.

Shadow Only. This option makes your clip invisible, displaying the Drop Shadow only.

As you get to a point where you need to add another keyframe, just drag your Vehicle in the **Monitor** to that **Position**, then make any other necessary adjustments to the clip's **Scale** and **Rotation**.

New keyframe points will automatically be added to the **Applied Effects** panel timeline as you change each property's setting.

You can add as many keyframes as you need to create a smooth motion path. You can also tweak your keyframes – or even remove them completely – as you work.

- To manually add a keyframe point, click the diamond-shaped **Make New Keyframe** button to the right of an effect's or property's listing, as in the illustration on page 185.

- To remove a keyframe point, **right-click** on it in the **Applied Effects** panel timeline and select **Delete**. (You can even drag over several keyframes to select them and delete them all at once.)

- If the **CTI** is sitting right on top of a keyframe point – even if it has been moved to another point previously – any changes you make to the effect's settings will be updated in that keyframe point's settings. To "jump" the **CTI** from one keyframe point to another, use the **Next Keyframe** or **Previous Keyframe** buttons to the right of the effect or property listing, as in the illustration.

Chapter 14
Cool Tricks with Titles
More than just words

Titles are more than just words on a page. They help to tell your story – and help your story come to life!

There are a number of fun things you can do with your titles. You can add or create cool animations for them. You can add effects that make them as exciting as your movie itself.

And, of course, you can recreate the most famous title sequence in movie history!

Text and titles can be treated like any other graphic. You can keyframe motion with them. You can add effects to them. You can even shape them and cut transparency through them.

Here are three of my favorite *Cool Tricks* for playing with words on the screen.

48 Create "Star Wars" Style Titles

It may be the most instantly recognizable titling effect in movie history. And, even though it's been parodied countless times, it's still a pretty exciting effect.

In addition to being remarkably easy to recreate!

You'll, of course, want an exciting outer space clip to use for your background. A great source for these types of photos is the NASA Web site. As with virtually all U.S. government-run sites, the photos and videos on this site are in the public domain and are free for you to use in any way you'd like (unless otherwise indicated on the site).

Check out these beautiful outer space photos at www.nasa.gov.

1 Add a background to Video 1

Drag your Starfield background clip from your **Project Assets** panel to the Video 1 track.

2 Create a Title

Position the **CTI** playhead back at the beginning of the clip, then select **New Text/Default Text** from the **Text** menu at the top of the program's interface.

A title clip will be added to your timeline, at the **CTI's** position, directly above your Starfield background and the Premiere Elements **Title Adjustments** workspace will open.

3 Set up your text style

To give yourself room to work, I recommend setting up your font and text size ahead of time.

The ideal font for the "Star Wars" scroll is Franklin Gothic Book. If that one isn't available on your computer, you can probably get away with Arial or Myriad Pro.

Set the font size to 33 point.
Select the **Center Justified** paragraph style.

Create "Star Wars" Style Titles

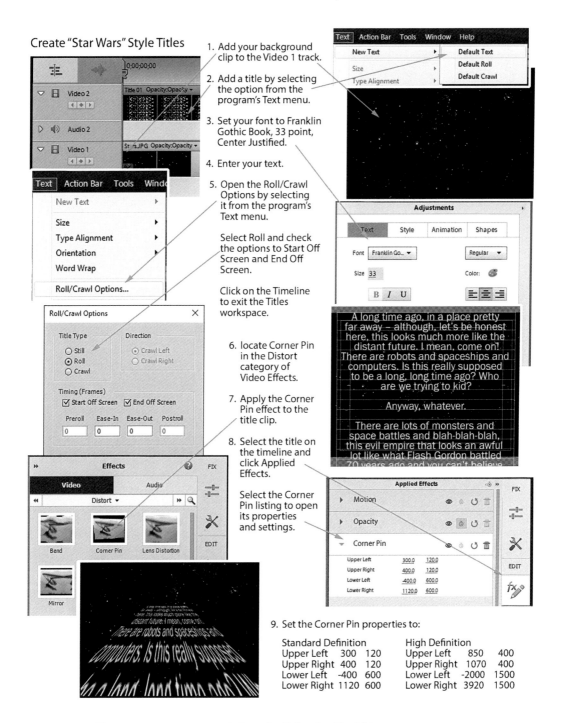

1. Add your background clip to the Video 1 track.

2. Add a title by selecting the option from the program's Text menu.

3. Set your font to Franklin Gothic Book, 33 point, Center Justified.

4. Enter your text.

5. Open the Roll/Crawl Options by selecting it from the program's Text menu.

   Select Roll and check the options to Start Off Screen and End Off Screen.

   Click on the Timeline to exit the Titles workspace.

6. locate Corner Pin in the Distort category of Video Effects.

7. Apply the Corner Pin effect to the title clip.

8. Select the title on the timeline and click Applied Effects.

   Select the Corner Pin listing to open its properties and settings.

9. Set the Corner Pin properties to:

	Standard Definition			High Definition	
Upper Left	300	120	Upper Left	850	400
Upper Right	400	120	Upper Right	1070	400
Lower Left	-400	600	Lower Left	-2000	1500
Lower Right	1120	600	Lower Right	3920	1500

You may even want to switch to the **Selection Tool** (the arrow **Mode** option under the **Text** tab on the **Adjustments** panel) and drag the text block to the top of the panel so you've got plenty of room to write.

To switch back to title text edit mode, click on the "T" or double-click on the text block.

4   Type in your text

The more convoluted the better. Remember, this effect has been done so often that it works best as parody.

As an alternative to typing in the **Title Adjustments** workspace, you can type all of your text in Microsoft Word or OpenOffice Writer. Copy it (by selecting it and pressing **Ctrl+c**) and paste it into your **Titles** text block (by positioning your cursor inside the text block and pressing **Ctrl+v**).

For best results, keep your text to less than 35 characters per line.

Don't worry if your text runs off the bottom of the **Monitor** panel.

5   Set the title up as a roll

While still in the **Title Adjustments** workspace, go to the program's **Text** menu and select **Roll/Crawl Options.**

On the **Roll/Crawl Options** screen, select the **Roll** option, and check the options to set the clip to both **Start Off Screen** and **End Off Screen.**

HOT TIP
Ligatures

A little attention to detail can mean the subtle difference between great-looking titles and titles that look amateurish and careless.

Selecting a good font can make a big difference. Professional fonts like Helvetica, Myriad Pro, Garamond Pro, Franklin Gothic and the old favorite Trajan make a much better impression than silly or showy fonts like Comic Sans, Fat and various Script fonts.

Additionally, using true ligatures instead of typewritery symbols can greatly improve the look of your titles. Using ligatures means the difference between using true quotation marks (" ") and using amateurish-looking tick marks (" ").

In Windows, the easiest way to get true ligatures is to use Alt key combinations. To type an Alt key combination, hold down the Alt key and type the number that follows. When you release the Alt key, the ligature will appear.

Here are some useful Alt key combinations:

| Apostrophe | Alt 0146 | Open Quotes | Alt 0147 | Close Quotes | Alt 0148 |
| Bullet | Alt 0149 | "M" Dash | Alt 0150 | | |

Monetary prefixes for non-U.S. currency as well as accented letters can also be produced by Alt key combinations. Ted Montgomery's site offers a great list of Alt key combinations:

www.tedmontgomery.com/tutorial/altchrc.html

To close the **Title Adjustments** workspace and return to normal editing mode, click on the **Adjust** button on the right side of the program or simply click on the timeline.

6   Locate the Corner Pin effect

Click the **Effects** button on the program's **Toolbar**.

The **Corner Pin** effect is located in the **Distort** category of **Video Effects**.

7   Apply the Corner Pin to your title

Drag the **Corner Pin** effect onto your title clip on the timeline.

8   Open the title's Applied Effects panel

With the title clip selected on your timeline, click the **Applied Effects** button on the right side of the program.

The title's **Applied Effects** panel will open.

9   Set the Corner Pin's positions

Click on the **Corner Pin** listing on the **Applied Effects** panel to open the effect's properties and settings.

For 720x480 video, set the locations of each corner point as follows:

Upper Left	300	120
Upper Right	400	120
Lower Left	-400	600
Lower Right	1120	600

For 1920x1080 high-definition video, use these settings:

Upper Left	850	400
Upper Right	1070	400
Lower Left	-2000	1500
Lower Right	3920	1500

You will likely need to render your video (by pressing the **Enter** key) before you will be able to see a good, clean playback of your effect.

It also may go by a lot faster than you expect. Remember, the **Roll/Crawl** effect's speed is based on the length of the clip. So, to slow down your title roll, drag the end of your title to extend its length on your timeline.

Depending on how long your text runs, you may want to extend it to 20, 30 seconds or longer.

Finally, if you'd like, you can even add a fade out at the end of the roll so that the titles seem to drifting off into space. To add a fade at the end of the clip, right-click on your title on the timeline and select the **Fade Out Video** option.

49 Create a Custom Title Animation

You're not by any means limited to the **Roll/Crawl** effect for creating interesting ways for your titles to move on and off your screen.

With some simple keyframing tricks, you can create pretty much any kind of animation for your titles you can imagine.

Here is a basic fly-in/pause/fly-out title animation. In other words, your title will fly in from the left, pause for a few seconds so that your audience can read it, then fly off-screen to the right.

1   **Create a Title**

Position the **CTI** playhead back at the point on your timeline at which you'd like your title to appear, then select **New Text/ Default Text** from the **Text** menu at the top of the program's interface.

A title clip will be added to your timeline, at the **CTI's** position, and the Premiere Elements **Title Adjustments** workspace will open.

2   **Create your title**

Type over the default **Add Text** to create your title.

Set your font size to about 66 points. We'll want this title to appear in just a corner of your video frame.

HOT TIP
Safe Margins

If you **right-click** on the **Monitor** panel, you will find the option to turn on the **Safe Margins**. These **Safe Margins** appear over your video frame as a pair of concentric rectangular overlays (as illustrated at the top of the next page).

Televisions, even the newest models, have a tendency to cut the edges off your video frame. This is nothing you can prevent. The purpose of **Safe Margins**, then, is to indicate to you the area of your video frame that you can be assured will always be visible on any TV screen.

We recommend that, any time you create titles, you work with these margins turned on, and that you ensure that your titles remain within the inner **Text Safe** rectangular margin. This will prevent such embarrassments as your title "Gone With the Wind" appearing on some TVs as "one With the Win."

Create a Custom Title Animation

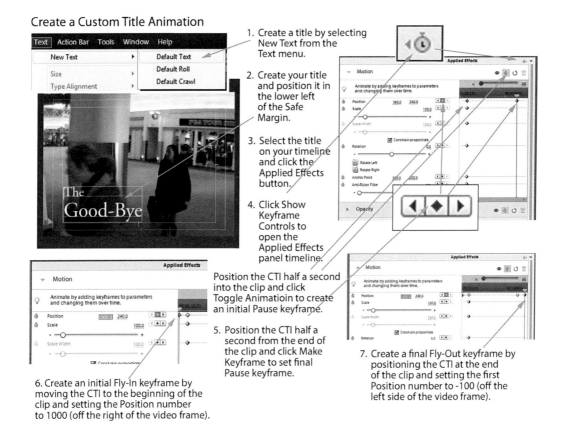

1. Create a title by selecting New Text from the Text menu.

2. Create your title and position it in the lower left of the Safe Margin.

3. Select the title on your timeline and click the Applied Effects button.

4. Click Show Keyframe Controls to open the Applied Effects panel timeline.

Position the CTI half a second into the clip and click Toggle Animatioin to create an initial Pause keyframe.

5. Position the CTI half a second from the end of the clip and click Make Keyframe to set final Pause keyframe.

6. Create an initial Fly-In keyframe by moving the CTI to the beginning of the clip and setting the Position number to 1000 (off the right of the video frame).

7. Create a final Fly-Out keyframe by positioning the CTI at the end of the clip and setting the first Position number to -100 (off the left side of the video frame).

When you're done typing, switch to the **Selection Tool** (the arrow **Mode** option under the **Text** tab on the **Adjustments** panel) and drag your title to the lower left corner of the **Title Safe Margin** of your video frame.

To close the **Title Adjustments** workspace and return to normal editing mode, click on the **Adjust** button on the right side of the program or simply click on the timeline.

3   Open the title's Applied Effects panel

With the title selected on your timeline, click the **Applied Effects** button on the right side of the program.

The title's **Applied Effects** panel will open.

Since the title is already in the position we'd like it to be in for the "pause" segment of its animation, the first thing we'll do is add a keyframe point to lock it in position.

4   Set your first Pause keyframe

Click the **Motion** listing on the **Applied Effects** panel to open the effect's properties and settings.

Click the **Show Keyframe Controls** button (the stopwatch) on the upper right of the panel to open the **Applied Effects** panel timeline.

Position the **CTI** playhead on the **Applied Effects** panel timeline about half a second in from the beginning of the title clip.

Click the **Toggle Animation** button, as illustrated on page 195. A set of keyframe points will be created at the position of the **CTI** on the **Applied Effects** panel timeline.

5 **Set a final Pause keyframe**

Move the **CTI** on the **Applied Effects** panel timeline to about half a second before the end of the title clip.

Click the diamond-shaped **Make Keyframe** button to the right of the **Position** settings. A keyframe point will appear at the position of the **CTI** representing the current **Position** settings.

6 **Set the initial Fly-In keyframe**

Move the **CTI** to the beginning of the title clip on the **Applied Effects** panel timeline.

Change the first number listed after **Position** (the horizontal vector) to 1000–2000 for high-definition (or whatever moves your title completely off the right side of your video frame).

A new **Position** keyframe will automatically be added at the **CTI's** position.

HOT TIP
Optimizing your timeline view

Because video and audio tracks are added together to your timeline, you may find your timeline's vertical space expanding unmanageably as you add tracks. You can streamline the look of your timeline by removing unnecessary tracks from your view.

All of these options are available when you **right-click** on a blank area on your timeline:

Delete Empty Tracks hides all tracks that do not include audio or video clips (except the default Audio 1, Narration and Soundtrack audio tracks).

Unchecking **Audio Tracks** hides all audio tracks, except for the default tracks.

Track Size sets the vertical width of your video and audio tracks.

7 **Set the final Fly-Out keyframe**

Move the **CTI** to the end of the title clip.

Set the first number listed after **Position** to -100 or whatever moves your clip off the left side of your video frame.

And that's all there is to it!

When you play your video, your title should now fly in from the right side of the screen, pause for four seconds, then fly off the left side of the screen.

COOL TRICK

50 Create a "Light Ray" Title Effect

This titling effect combines several Premiere Elements tricks, a little keyframing and three tracks of video – but the result is well worth the effort.

The effect will be as if your title were resting on a reflective surface, a light source moving behind it, sending bright rays of light through a fog, out and around your text.

Let your friends try to guess how you did it!

1 **Create a Title**

Position the **CTI** playhead back at the point on your timeline at which you'd like your title to appear, then select **New Text/Default Text** from the **Text** menu at the top of the program's interface.

A title clip will be added to your timeline, at the **CTI's** position, and the Premiere Elements **Title Adjustments** workspace will open.

2 **Create your title**

Type over the default **Add Text** to create your title.

I recommend you use a heavy font or bold font style. (Adobe Garamond Pro Bold works well.) And this effect works best when your text is a single line long, as in the illustration.

The default white color will work fine.

Click on the **Selection Tool** (the arrow in the **Mode** options) and position your title so that it is centered horizontally and rests just above the vertical center of the video frame.

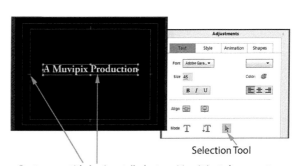

Selection Tool

Center your title horizontally, but position it just above center vertically, so that the bottom of the title sits right on the vertical center.

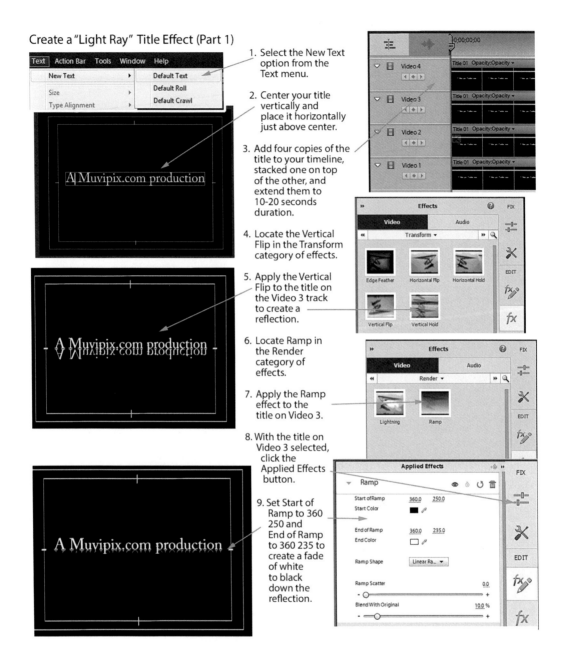

Create a "Light Ray" Title Effect (Part 1)

1. Select the New Text option from the Text menu.

2. Center your title vertically and place it horizontally just above center.

3. Add four copies of the title to your timeline, stacked one on top of the other, and extend them to 10-20 seconds duration.

4. Locate the Vertical Flip in the Transform category of effects.

5. Apply the Vertical Flip to the title on the Video 3 track to create a reflection.

6. Locate Ramp in the Render category of effects.

7. Apply the Ramp effect to the title on Video 3.

8. With the title on Video 3 selected, click the Applied Effects button.

9. Set Start of Ramp to 360 250 and End of Ramp to 360 235 to create a fade of white to black down the reflection.

To close the **Title Adjustments** workspace and return to normal editing mode, click on the **Adjust** button on the right side of the program or simply click on the timeline.

3   Add three copies of your title to the timeline

Drag your title from the **Project Assets** panel to the Video 2 track, the Video 3 track and the Video 4 track – so that the four copies of the title are stacked on top of one another.

If your timeline does not yet have four video tracks, simply drag your title or clip to the blank area directly above an existing video track. When you release your mouse button, a new video track will be created and your clip will be placed in it.

Line up all four video tracks so that they all begin and end at the same point.

Because this video effect is most effective if it takes a while to roll out, drag the ends of each title clip so that all four extend to a duration of 10-20 seconds on your timeline.

4   Locate the Vertical Flip effect

Click the **Effects** button on the program's **Toolbar**.

Vertical Flip is in the **Transform** category of **Video Effects**.

5   Apply Vertical Flip to Video 3

Select the clip on the Video 3 track and drag **Vertical Flip** onto it.

You should see an upside-down reflection of your title appear directly beneath it on your **Monitor** panel.

6   Locate the Ramp effect

To give the impression that the upside-down title is a reflection of the title, apply the **Ramp** effect to it. The **Ramp** effect will make this title look whiter at the top and then fade off to black at the bottom.

The **Ramp** effect is in the **Render** category of **Video Effects**.

7   Apply the Ramp effect to Video 3

Drag the **Ramp** effect onto the title clip on Video 3.

8   Open Video 3's Applied Effects panel

With the title clip on Video 3 selected, click on the **Applied Effects** button on the right side of the program.

The title's **Applied Effects** panel will open.

9   Adjust the Ramp effect

Click on the **Ramp** listing in the **Applied Effects** panel to open its properties and settings.

For Standard Definition Video: For High Definition Video:

Set **Start of Ramp** to 360 250.   Set **Start of Ramp** to 960 600.
Set **End of Ramp** to 360 235.   Set **End of Ramp** to 960 400.

Set **Blend with Original** to 10%.

Naturally, you may need to tweak these numbers just a bit for your unique situation. But, basically, we've set the **Ramp** effect to make our upside-down title whitest at just before the vertical center of the video frame and then to fade off to black about 15 pixels below it. The result should be a pretty authentic-looking reflection for our title – lighter at the top and faded or darker at the bottom!

Next we'll create a light ray effect for one copy of our clip title by using the **Zoom Blur** effect on the title on the Video 2 track. Once it's done, we'll copy it onto the title clip on the Video 1 track.

10 Locate the Zoom Blur effect

Click the **Effects** button on the program's **Toolbar**.

The **Zoom Blur** is in the **NewBlue Art Effects** category of **Video Effects**.

11 Apply Zoom Blur to Video 2

Drag the **Zoom Blur** onto the title clip on Video 2.

Your text should appear to be glowing from as if lit through a fog by a light source behind it.

12 Open Video 2's Applied Effects panel

With the title on Video 2 selected, click the **Applied Effects** button on the right side of the program.

The title's **Applied Effects** panel will open.

13 Adjust the Zoom Blur effect

Click on the **Zoom Blur** listing on the **Applied Effects** panel to open the effect's properties settings.

Set **Zoom** and **Blend** both to 100%.

Our title should now appears to have a cool glow, as if light is shining through a fog behind it. Our next step is to use keyframing to create the effect of the light source behind our title moving from the left to right side of the video frame.

14 Set an initial Zoom Blur keyframe

Click the **Show Keyframe Controls** button in the upper right of the panel to open the **Applied Effects** panel timeline.

Move the **CTI** playhead on the **Applied Effects** panel timeline to the beginning of the clip.

Set the **Center** vector numbers for the **Zoom Blur** effect to 125 240 (or whatever makes it appear that the center of the **Zoom Blur** is directly behind the first letter in your title).

Create a "Light Ray" Title Effect (Part 2)

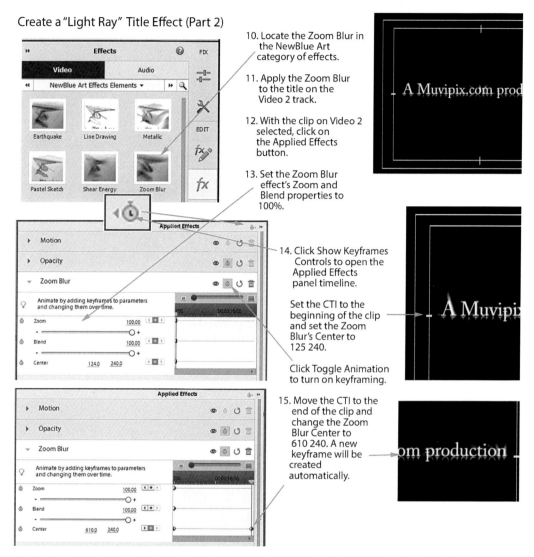

10. Locate the Zoom Blur in the NewBlue Art category of effects.

11. Apply the Zoom Blur to the title on the Video 2 track.

12. With the clip on Video 2 selected, click on the Applied Effects button.

13. Set the Zoom Blur effect's Zoom and Blend properties to 100%.

14. Click Show Keyframes Controls to open the Applied Effects panel timeline.

Set the CTI to the beginning of the clip and set the Zoom Blur's Center to 125 240.

Click Toggle Animation to turn on keyframing.

15. Move the CTI to the end of the clip and change the Zoom Blur Center to 610 240. A new keyframe will be created automatically.

The keyframed Zoom Blur will create an animated effect in which the center of the blur – the center of our light ray effect – will begin behind the first letter in our title and then move down the words, ending behind the last letter of our title.

For high-definition video, use a **Center** vector more like 270 540.

In other words, it should look as if the light shining through fog is now behind the first letter in our title.

Click the **Toggle Animation** button (stopwatch icon) to the right of the **Zoom Blur** listing in the **Applied Effects** panel to begin your keyframing session.

A set of diamond-shaped keyframes will be added to the **Applied Effects** panel timeline at the position of the **CTI**.

15   Set a final Zoom Blur keyframe

Move the **CTI** to the end of the clip on the **Applied Effects** panel timeline.

Set the **Center** vector numbers to 610 240 (or whatever puts the center of the **Zoom Blur** directly behind the last letter in your title. (For high-definition video, set the **Center** vector to 1650 540.)

A new keyframe point will automatically be added for the **Center** property at the position of the **CTI**.

When you play your clip or scrub through it (dragging the **CTI** back and forth) it should appear that the foggy light source behind your title moves from the left to the right side of your title.

To speed up the motion of this effect, drag the keyframe points on the **Applied Effects** panel timeline closer together. To slow the effect, move the keyframe points farther apart (extending the lengths of your title clips on your timeline if necessary).

Now that we've created a keyframed effect for the title clip on the Video 2 track, we can use **Paste Effects and Adjustments** to apply the very same animated glow effect and keyframing to the title clip on Video 1.

16   Copy the effects from Video 2

Right-click on the title clip on the Video 2 track on your timeline and select **Copy**.

HOT TIP
Copying vs. duplicating a title

The are a number of ways to make more than one copy of a title clip for your project. However, they do have quite the same results.

When you create a copy of a title by using **Copy & Paste** (either on the timeline or in the **Project Assets** panel) or by dragging the same title to your timeline several times, you not only create a copy of your title, you create a *clone* of it. This means that whatever changes you make to one copy of this title will also be made to *all* copies of it. This is not usually how you want your titles to behave.

If you want to reuse a title (using it as a template for other titles, for instance) and you do not want the changes you make to one copy to affect all copies, you should *duplicate* rather than copy the title. To duplicate a title, **right-click** on it in the **Project Assets** panel and select the **Duplicate** option.

A duplicate of a title can be edited or revised and those changes will not be reflected in any other copy of the title.

Create a "Light Ray" Title Effect (Part 3)

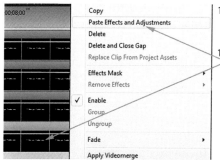

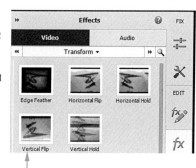

16. Right-click on the title clip on Video 2 and select Copy.

17. Right-click on the title clip on Video 1 and select Paste Effects and Adjustments. The effects and keyframing will be copied from the Video 2 clip to the Video 1 clip.

18. Locate the Vertical Flip in the Transform category of effects.

19. Apply Vertical Flip to the title clip on Video 1 to make it appear to be the reflection of the light ray effect.

The final product will be a title that seems to be resting on a reflective surface as a white light, shining through fog, moves from the left to right side behind it.

The effect can be enhanced by adding color to one or more of the title clips and by raising the height of the Zoom Blur clips.

17 Paste Effects and Adjustments to Video 1

Right-click on the title clip on the Video 1 track and select **Paste Effects and Adjustments**.

The effects and keyframing created for the title clip on Video 2 will be applied to the title clip on Video 1. In your **Monitor**, it will appear that the **Zoom Blur** effect has been intensified.

Now all that remains is for you to flip the title clip on the Video 1 track so that your keyframed, foggy lighting effect appears as part of the reflection.

18 Again locate the Vertical Flip effect

Click the **Effects** button on the program's **Toolbar**.

Vertical Flip is in the **Transform** category of **Video Effects**.

19 Apply Vertical Flip to Video 1

Drag the **Vertical Flip** effect onto the title clip on Video 1.

You should see the same keyframed **Zoom Blur** "foggy light" effect appearing as part of the title's reflection.

You may want to render this clip (by pressing the **Enter** key on your keyboard) before you play it to see it in all of its glory. It's really an amazing effect, and a perfect special effect for creating a very cool movie title or a logo for your production company.

There are some interesting ways to intensify the effect, if you'd like.

- One way to intensify the effect it to increase the height of the foggy light rays in our **Zoom Blur** effect. Open the **Applied Effects** panel for the title clip on the Video 3 track and then click the **Motion** properties. Uncheck the **Uniform Scale** checkbox under the **Scale** property and raise the **Scale Height**.

- Although we've kept the vertical **Center** position (the second number) of our **Zoom Blur** pretty much along the middle of the video frame (240 in a 480 pixel high NTSC frame or 288 in a PAL 576 pixel high frame), you can create some interesting effects by raising or lowering these numbers also. Raising this vector number will make it looks like the light source behind your title is lower than your title; lower the number will make it look like the light source is higher than your title, shining down at it.

- You can also experiment with different effects by changing the color of your text. Open the **Title Adjustments** workspace for a clip by double-clicking on it on your timeline. In the **Title Adjustments** workspace, you can select the text and, clicking on the **Color Properties** button (the painter's palette), you can change the color of your blurred text. A cool blue or a fiery red can make your light ray effect even more dazzling!

- Finally, if you create a duplicate of your title clips (by **right-clicking** on the title in your **Project Assets** panel and selecting the **Duplicate** option), you can use it rather than copies of your clips to create this effect. The advantage of using a duplicate of your title rather than a copy is that you can open the **Title Adjustments** workspace for a duplicate and change its **Color Properties** and this change will only be applied to your duplicated title without affecting any other copy. (You can add, for instance, a blue foggy light behind your white title in one copy of the title only.)

Want to see our tricks in action?

Check out our Cool Tricks & Hot Tips page at Muvipix.com. We'll show you examples of some of the effects we create in this book as well as walk you through the process of creating a few more, step-by-step.

http://Muvipix.com/CoolTricks2018.php

And while you're there, drop by our Community Forum and say hello. We love watching our community grow!

122

Made in the USA
Middletown, DE
07 December 2017